MW01659841

The Johns Hopkins Hospital Reports, Volume 1...

Johns Hopkins Hospital

THE JOHNS HOPKINS HOSPITAL REPORTS

MONOGRAPHS. NEW SERIES No. 1

FREE THROMBI AND BALL-THROMBI IN THE HEART

BY

J. H. HEWITT, M.D., Chicago, Ill.

Former Resident Pathologist, The Lakeside Hospital, Cleveland, Ohio

Illustrated—20 Figures

BALTIMORE

THE JOHNS HOPKINS PRESS

1913

CONTENTS.

FREE THROMBI AND BALL-THROMBI IN THE HEART.*

By J. H. HEWITT, M. D., Chicago, Ill.

Former Resident Pathologist, The Lakeside Hospital, Cleveland, Ohio.

Within the last one hundred years there have been, according to my investigation of the literature, over 30 cases of loose bodies found in the cavities of the heart on post mortem examinations. These bodies may be divided, according to their composition, into two general classes: (I.) Those consisting of material different from any of the existing elements of the blood or substances that may be directly derived from those elements, as emboli of tumor cells;[1] (II.) those made up of elements derived from the blood, as thrombi and ante mortem blood clots. I have left unconsidered all cases of the first class in this paper, but of the cases in the second class I have endeavored to find and to consult the original report in all.

It has heretofore been the custom of authors to consider these loose thrombi found in the heart in a general way and to class them all under the heading "ball-thrombi." A careful consideration of the original reports of many, in fact, the majority of these cases, shows that, so far as can be made out from the description or the accompanying illustrations, the thrombi were not "balls," but more or less irregular ante mortem blood clots. Accordingly, this second class of loose bodies in the heart may be considered under two subheadings: (a) those loose thrombi of irregular shape, size, and situation, associated with a constant pathological change in the heart, or, in other words, free thrombi, and (b) ball-thrombi.

I have herewith first reviewed the literature on free thrombi of whatever character found in the heart. I have one additional case to add, and have been able to collect fairly complete reports on three other cases that are incompletely described, or only mentioned, in the literature; and one case that has not been before published has been referred to me and I include it also.

In 1814 William Wood,[2] of Edinburgh, reported, in a letter to the editor of the *Edinburgh Medical and Surgical Journal,* the first

* Read by title at the meeting of The American Association of Pathologists and Bacteriologists, Chicago, April, 1911.

genuine case of "ball-thrombus of the heart." This is practically 70 years before either those cases mentioned by v. Recklinghausen, to whom all the German authors that have written on the subject have given the credit for reporting the first case, or the spurious case of Macleod, which had a marked notoriety, were published. His description is so precise and his opinion as to how these bodies are formed, in a general way, conforms so nearly to those advanced by much later writers that I here include the greater part of his paper verbatim.

Letter inclosing history and dissection of a case, in which a foreign body was found within the heart, to Dr. Duncan, Jr., by William Wood, Fellow of the Royal College of Surgeons, Edinburgh.

Dear Sir:—I enclose an account of the principal symptoms of disease which occurred in a young girl who died, under the care of my father and myself, in consequence of an affection of the heart, together with a description of the morbid appearances discovered on dissection.

The symptoms and progress of the disease in this girl, you will perceive, differ little from those generally met with in cases where there has been found, after death, such an alteration in the structure of the heart, or of the large vessels arising from it, as must have disturbed the regularity of the circulation of the blood through that organ; the dissection, however, appears to me to be a singular and interesting one, from its affording an example, by no means of frequent occurrence, I believe, of the formation, during life, and existence for probably a great time, of loose substances, of considerable size, within one of the cavities of the heart.

All the symptoms of the disease, as well as the morbid appearances of the right cavities of the heart, may be, I think, satisfactorily explained on the principle of obstruction to the free passage of the blood through the left side of that organ; and, indeed, the principal difficulty in the case seems to be in conceiving how the circulation should have been sufficiently carried on to maintain life for any length of time, under such a degree of obstruction as must have been produced in this instance by the joint effect of the diseased mitral valves and of the foreign bodies contained in the left auricle, the former materially contracting the opening between the auricle and ventricle, and the latter retarding and diminishing the current of blood toward it; an effect which, from their situation, size, and form, these substances seem to have been well calculated to produce.

With regard to the morbid appearances on the left side of the heart the most probable supposition appears to me to be that the disease had originally existed in the mitral valves, producing diminution in the size of the ventricular openings; that, in consequence of this contraction, accumulation of blood had taken place in the left auricle, and coagula had been there formed, upon which coagulable lymph had been afterwards slowly and gradually deposited; the different substances thus formed assuming different shapes according to the relative situations in which they had been placed with regard to each other, and to the internal parts of the auricle. But whether this be or be not a true account of the formation of these solid bodies, there can be no doubt, I think, from their laminated structure, that they had existed during life.

Unfortunately in this, as in all other cases of organic affections of the heart, neither the history of the disease, nor the examination of the body after death, affords us any practical information whatever; if, however, the case appears to you worthy of being recorded as an object of curiosity, I request that it may be inserted in your Journal.

Yours sincerely, W. Wood.

A. S., a girl of 15 years of age, who had been always of rather a delicate habit, about three years ago, when walking along the street, became suddenly affected with great difficulty of breathing, and general weakness, and was so unwell that it was with difficulty she could continue her walk home. Next day she was rather better, but ever afterwards remained subject to difficulty of breathing on taking any violent exercise. In addition to this complaint she, soon after the first attack, became affected with constant strong pulsation in the region of the heart, much increased on walking up stairs or climbing an ascent. It was at this time that I was first called to see her. I found her complaining very much of uneasiness in the chest, from the constant palpitation; she could not bear her clothes at all tight, and she seemed very uncomfortable when the hand was pressed at all tightly on the thorax. The palpitation was so strong that it could be distinctly seen at a considerable distance. On applying the hand over the region of the heart strong palpitation was felt; and at a particular spot, about the size of a crown piece, a peculiar thrilling sensation was communicated to the fingers at each stroke of the heart, not easily described but somewhat resembling the effect produced on the ear by the emission of a short hissing sound at frequent regular intervals. She could lie in bed, but her sleep was disturbed by disagreeable dreams. These complaints gradually increased in severity, with the addition of fainting-fits of some duration, occurring generally three or four times in the course of every day. These were sometimes so sudden in their attack that she dropped down instantly, deprived of sense and motion; at other times, according to her friends' account, they were preceded by an involuntary contraction of the fingers and toes. These fainting-fits continued for upwards of two months, when they left her, and never again returned. Being removed to the country, I had no opportunity of seeing her for some time, but I was informed that while there, having spit up a considerable quantity of a clear watery fluid, after a severe fit of coughing, she had become considerably easier, and could take a little gentle exercise, which she had not been able to do when she left town. On her return, I found her certainly rather easier, but the strong palpitation was still constantly present. This state of comparative comfort, however, was of short duration, for very soon the symptoms became all much aggravated, with the addition of frequent spitting of blood, though in no great quantity. She was now unable to lie down, but was supported in bed by means of pillows, in nearly an upright posture. The pulse was intermittent. She had a very sallow complexion, and was extremely out of spirits. She lingered on, gradually and slowly losing strength and flesh, till the beginning of November, when she died quite exhausted, above three years from the commencement of her complaints. For many weeks previous to her death, dropsical effusion had taken place into the cellular substance of the lower extremities, and, by her friends' account, for about fifteen or sixteen days, large purple spots, of the size of half-crown pieces, had appeared on different parts of her body.

During her illness digitalis was repeatedly administered, occasionally with the effect of procuring temporary relief; the rest of the treatment consisted in regulating the diet, attending to the state of the bowels, and in occasionally exhibiting cordials.

Dissection.—Within the general cavity of the thorax there was found a very considerable quantity of bloody serum. The lungs in general were of a healthy appearance, but towards the root of one of the left lobes, there was discovered a considerable mass of a white gritty concretion.

The pericardium, which was somewhat thickened, being laid open, several ounces of clear serum were removed, and the heart brought into view, considerably larger in size than natural, the increase appearing most remarkable on the right side, the cavities of which, particularly the auricle, were much distended with blood. The heart being removed from the body, with the view of having it particularly examined, the right auricle and ventricle were laid open; in these the disease seemed to be entirely confined to enlargement of their cavities. The tricuspid and semilunar valves of the pulmonary artery were apparently in a sound state.

On splitting open the left auricle, which appeared larger than usual, the musculi pectinati were observed to be considerably increased in thickness, and there was found occupying, and nearly entirely filling up, the cavity of the left sinus venosus, a round firm body of considerable size; immediately under which, and over the situation of the opening into the ventricle, there was contained another solid substance of an oval form. A third substance, rough and irregular, had also been lodged in the auricle, but its situation could not be precisely ascertained; it lay, however, towards the ventricular opening. All these being removed, an attempt was made to pass the finger from the auricle into the ventricle, but this was found to be impossible. The left ventricle was therefore fully laid open by an incision, and, on examining the mitral valves, they were found to be much thickened, and quite opake, by their connection and situation permanently contracting the opening from the auricle into a small oval fissure, into which not even the tip of the little finger could be introduced.

The semilunar valves of the aorta were opake, and much thickened.

The substance, occupying the sinus venosus of the left auricle, when particularly examined, was found to be of a darkish red color, in form completely spherical, measuring rather more than an inch and a half in diameter. It felt firm, but elastic; the surface was everywhere smooth and polished, but having a singularly clotted appearance. It had no connection with the surrounding parts, rolling loosely in the auricle. When cut open, after having been kept for some days in diluted alcohol, it was found to consist of a sac, one-eighth of an inch in thickness, formed of an immense number of firm smooth laminæ, which could be easily separated from each other. Within the cavity formed by this sac was contained a quantity of coagulated blood. The flat substance which lay between the round body and the opening into the ventricle was of an oval form, an inch in length and three-fourths of an inch across at the widest part. Its upper surface was of the same smooth clotted appearance with that of the former, slightly concave, so as to form a kind of superficial socket for it to roll in; the under surface, which lay over the mitral valves, was rough and irregular, containing something somewhat resembling a firm coagulum of blood in a concave depression.

In 1856 Dr. Henry Cady[1] reported three cases of "Fibrinous bodies found in the heart after death." The third and last of these cases was briefly as follows:

"A male child, about two years old, always well till about nine months before, when it suffered from a slight attack of diarrhœa. Six months later it was seized with a genuine attack of dysentery, though of only medium intensity. The child was convalescent in two weeks from the onset of the disease. After a continued state of improvement for four or five days, suddenly, in the middle of the night, having rested quietly up to that time, it was suddenly seized with a convulsion, which lasted more than four hours. Twelve hours afterwards, however, it appeared nearly as well as before the fit. The night following it had a slight paroxysm lasting about five minutes; and on the night still succeeding, one still slighter, lasting no more than half a minute. There was no more appearance of convulsive action till nearly the close of the third day from the last named period, when it was seized with a fit more severe than the first, and continued profoundly convulsed for nearly 12 hours, when death closed the scene."

Post mortem examination, made 12 hours after death, showed patches of injected mucosa and ulcerations that had not healed in the colon; considerable congestion of the blood vessels of the brain. The heart appeared normal, some "lumps of dark-colored coagula in the left side of the heart. The right ventricle was clear. The right auricle contained a small amount of dark coagulum, and in addition a small body of fleshy color, rather solid, a trifle less than an inch in length and nearly half an inch thick, in shape cylindrical. It was found lying on the tricuspid valve. . . . . This body was subsequently examined microscopically and pronounced to be fibrin." His conclusion on the subject is, "that the substances were in the heart prior to, and were the cause of death."

In 1858 Van der Byl[4] reported to the Pathological Society of London a "case of sudden death from contraction of the mitral orifice, and its obstruction, produced by a globular vegetation detached from the left auricle." The patient was a woman who had suffered for twelve months from "shortness of breath, palpitation, frequent catarrh and troublesome cough." During the three weeks preceding death she had edema of the legs, ascites, orthopnea, and frequent cough. The heart's action was rather forcible, with a mitral regurgitant bruit. She had never had rheumatism. The urine was heavy with albumin, but contained no tube casts. After breakfast one morning she suddenly fainted, became insensible, and died in a few minutes.

On section the heart was found enlarged and hypertrophied, the left auricle contained "an irregular, shaggy-looking mass . . . . . sticking in the orifice of the mitral valve. This mass "floated in water" and "assumed a sac-like appearance. . . . . . The portions required to complete the sac or capsule were found adherent to the inner surface of the auricular appendix by means of fibrinous bands and processes, which were entwined in the musculi pectinati. Three or four smaller globular bodies about the size of peas were found in the left auricular appendix, similarly fixed. On squeezing one of these, it burst, and yielded a thick greyish, purulent-looking matter, which seemed to form the contents of a capsule, similar to but smaller than the one found detached in the auricle. . . . . There was no actual organic union between any of these coagula and the walls of the auricle. The mitral orifice was contracted to four-tenths of an inch in diameter and showed warty vegetations projecting from its free margins. The aortic valve leaflets were fenestrated. The endocardium of the posterior wall of the left ventricle showed a thickened "rough patch resembling a cicatrix, about the size of a shilling." Brain, normal; no emboli in its vessels. Lungs showed infarcts the size of a hen's egg, as well as the spleen and kidneys. The latter were granular and possessed small cysts. The liver was "nodulated and granular, and on section presented radiating patches of extravasated blood." In his remarks on the case he expresses the opinion that these coagula arise from the impeded circulation caused by the contracted mitral orifice and they owe their situation in the appendix to the fact that "it is furthest from the circulating current." The chief interest is, he thinks, in "the mode in which fibrinous coagula in the heart may produce death."

In 1863 Dr. Jno. W. Ogle[1] reported briefly to the Pathological Society of London the history and post mortem findings of a case. His report is accompanied by an admirable picture of the condition, showing the case to be undoubtedly as described, and also a few remarks which demonstrate clearly that he had the correct conception of the mode of formation of these bodies. His case is as follows:

Female, age 43, admitted into St. George's Hospital, complaining of dyspnœa and anasarca, of which she had been suffering for six weeks, as well as a feeble and irregular action of the heart. Examination with the stethoscope revealed mucous râles all over the chest, egophony on the right side, a loud bruit, audible at the apex of the heart, heard distinctly with systole, doubtfully with diastole. The patient was cupped on the chest and given diuretics. No albumin was found in the urine. She improved for a time, but gradually the breathing became more hurried, with no pain however, till finally the patient died five weeks after admission.

The autopsy showed the lungs edematous, their lower parts hepatized, a quantity of fluid in the right pleural cavity. "The heart was larger than ordinary and its walls thinned. The mitral valve was reduced by thickening, and by calcareous deposits in its elements to a small buttonhole shaped aperture. The inner surface of the left auricle had several patches of fibrin attached to it; and lying loose within its cavity was a large spherical mass or concretion of fibrin weighing rather more than four drachms (Fig. I), perfectly solid throughout, and uniformly granulated in a remarkable manner on its surface, except in two places, where marks, like undulations, existed. This globular mass had also attached to it at one spot a small amount of shreddy loose fibrin. Section through this singular body showed its interior to be mainly composed of friable fibrin; but, at one part, its circumference and a certain amount also of its inner substance was formed of distinctly laminated and darker colored fibrin." (The specimen exists as a preparation in the St. George's Hospital Pathological Museum, Series VI.)

The kidneys were large, coagulated, and contained "fibrinous blocks" (probably infarcts). The suprarenals were normal in size, but as firm almost as cartilage.

In his remarks on the case he suggests that this body was no doubt produced by "the constant and free agitation of a fragment of fibrinous coagulum separated from some part of the endocardium, and uniformly increased by fresh material at its circumference, precipitated from the surrounding blood-stream. The globular form having once been assumed, its continuance during the further increase of the con-

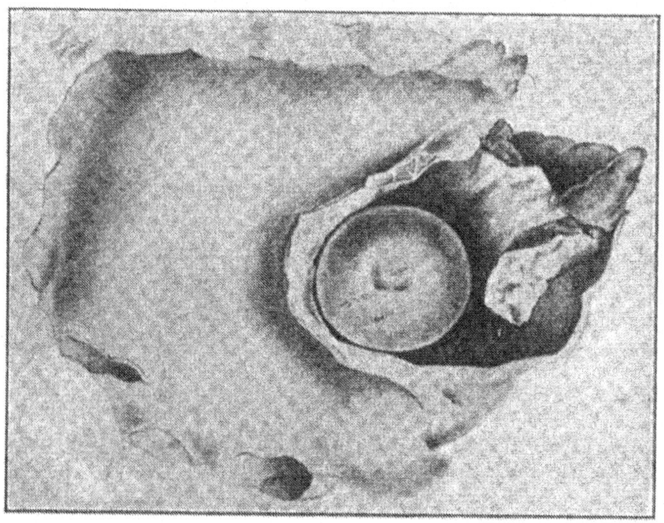

FIG. 1.—OGLE'S CASE.
A fibrinous concretion of a globular form lying loose within the left auricle of the heart.

cretion would easily be ensured." He also is at a loss to understand how the patient continued to live as long as she did, considering the presence of this "loose body" and the narrowed condition of the mitral valve; however, as we shall mention later, it was really the narrowed condition of the valve that probably caused the formation of the thrombus.

In 1878 J. Wickham Legg* reported to the Pathological Society of London "Two cases of loose balls of fibrin in the left auricle with mitral stenosis." The first case was as follows:

A young man, 22 years of age, brought dead to St. Bartholomew's Hospital by the police; nothing known as to the manner of his death.

The autopsy showed a well-nourished body, no edema, face slightly cyanotic, left sided chronic adhesive pleurisy with one orange-size pleural cyst. "The heart is very large and dilated in all four cavities; the right ventricle thickened and tough. No disease of the tricuspid and pulmonary valves. On opening the left auricle, which is greatly dilated, two balls of fibrin, clearly ante mortem coagula, fall out of the auricle. They are grey and granular on the surface and marked by lines resembling the impression made by a wave on the sandy shore. Both are about the same size, that of a pullet's egg, and irregularly oval, about 15 mm. long by 30 mm. broad. The auricular appendix holds a very firm adherent, almost cartilaginous clot which shows a broken-off end projecting into the auricle. It is quite possible that one of the balls may have been joined with this clot in the auricular appendage by a pedicle, as one of them shows a surface which closely corresponds to this broken-off end. The mitral orifice is a mere chink; it scarcely admits the tip of a man's forefinger. It is beset with granulations. . . . .

"Both lungs are edematous, red and firm; spleen, large, red and firm; liver nutmeggy; kidney normal size, congested. Aorta tolerably free from atheroma but narrowed."

He then expresses the opinion that such a concretion in the heart may act as a ball valve and was very probably the cause of death in this case. He mentions Van der Byl's case as a supporting argument. The thing that most perplexed him was how the ball managed to attain such a size before death ensued. He mentions Ogle's case and then reports the following case, which he credits to Dr. Gee, as examples where the manner of death was slow.

A woman, age 43, had been in St. Bartholomew's Hospital for 15 days when she died.

On section there was no anasarca; the lungs were collapsed and the heart was enlarged, about equally on both sides; the right ventricle was dilated and hypertrophied, and the left ventricle dilated but not hypertrophied; the left auricle was greatly dilated. "The mitral orifice is markedly contracted, so as not to admit more than the tip of the finger. In the left auricle there is a round ball about an inch and a half in diameter, very elastic, very smooth, and without any trace of pedicle; that is, altogether free in the cavity." The other valves were normal. There were emboli in the kidney.

"The mode of origin of these balls of fibrin," he says, "seems very easy of explanation. In the first place there must be a considerable amount of mitral stenosis. Then a clot forms in some part of the vascular system between the radicles of the pulmonary veins and the mitral orifice; in some cases, as in the first of these, a clot is found in the auricular appendix, or, perhaps, a pulmonary infarction leading to the formation of a secondary clot in the pulmonary veins. A part of this clot, too large to pass through the mitral orifice, is broken off and therefore remains in the left auricle, instead of passing into the general system of arteries and causing infarctions of different organs, as in an unnarrowed mitral orifice might take place. Pent in the left auricle, the clot, at first of an irregular shape, is generally overlaid with fresh layers of fibrin and, from the tendency to become round which bodies possess, the clot gradually assumes a spheroidal shape."

This report of Legg's appeared five years before v. Recklinghausen published his cases, but neither he nor any of the German authors have mentioned any English case except that of Macleod.

In 1883 Macleod[7] reported a case of "A movable clot in the right auricle." His case is briefly as follows:

A man, 27 years of age, while recovering from a thigh wound, was suddenly seized with "rice water" diarrhœa and vomiting which persisted for two days and was then followed by an itching skin eruption. The patient seemed convalescent when on the fifth day he was seized with a convulsion and immediately lapsed into unconsciousness, dyspnœa, and cyanosis. A diagnosis of probable pulmonary embolism was made. Diarrhœa was persistent and involuntary, divergent squint was noted. The convulsive attack repeated itself in the evening. From it he never recovered consciousness. He had quiet delirium on the 6th day and died on the 7th day.

"On post mortem examination there were found several soft, small yellow ante mortem clots in the left side of the heart. In the right auricle was a very firm, almost cartilaginous, greyish yellow, movable clot, half as large again as a walnut, lying over the tricuspid orifice."

He thereupon expresses his belief that the first convulsive attack was brought on by a partial occlusion of the tricuspid valve by this clot; with the weakening of the heart action, the clot fell away and thus accounted for the period of improvement between the first and second attacks. He suggests that had he known the real condition he would have tilted the bed in an effort to displace the clot.

From the evidence here given we may be sure that this was not a case of ball-thrombus, and may reasonably doubt whether the clot present was the cause of death. However, the case is quoted as one of ball-thrombus by several of the German writers on this subject. I give it to make the review of the literature complete and that certain references may be more readily understood.

In 1883 v. Recklinghausen[8] in his "Handbuch der allgemeinen Pathologie des Kreislaufs und der Ernährung," in his discussion of phleboliths and venous thrombi, mentions that he had in two cases seen analogues of these bodies in the left cavity of the heart. These bodies were in both cases pale red in color, of the nature of thrombi and contained in their interior a small cavity. The mitral valve was contracted to a size smaller than the tip of the little finger. The thrombus was completely free, somewhat bulged out, but its surface was everywhere smooth. There was no pedicle, and no indication of a place where such had been attached. He believed this to be an indication that they had existed for a long time free in the blood and that they had grown by the application of new surface layers while they rolled around in the auricle. He believed they had existed first in the auricular appendix and had thereupon increased in size till they were too large to pass through the contracted mitral orifice. He gives no history with either one of the cases.

In 1885, following Hertz's[9] report of two cases of ball-thrombi and his discussion of their pathology, v. Recklinghausen[9] reviewed the subject and criticized rather severely some of Hertz's theories. He answers him sarcastically for not mentioning in two cases he had commented on in his "Handbuch der allgemeinen Pathologie des Kreislaufs und der Ernährung," which he considered the first cases mentioned in the literature. However, as shown by Welch,[10] both authors were in error on this point for having overlooked the cases of Wood, Ogle and Legg, reported in English literature. He repeats word for word his statement concerning the two cases of ball-thrombi mentioned in his book to show that Hertz's cases agreed in general with his and that he might repudiate the opinion as incorrect which Hertz's reasoning would tend to establish. He disagrees with Hertz concerning the method of formation and rounding of the ball from the loosened clot, which he accepts as the initial condition for the formation of the thrombus. This he argues is not at all one of grinding and smoothing off of rough edges and points with which the thrombus nucleus is at first covered, but rather a process of moulding, as potter's clay, rolling, and the application of new layers, and is similar to the method of formation of renal and gall stones. As to whether this thrombus can act as a ball-valve and suddenly occlude the valvular orifice, is a point on which he cannot agree with Hertz and shows the unreasonableness of his conjecture in comparison with the autopsy and clinical findings of Hertz's two cases. He notes that the funnel-shaped mitral orifices are most commonly oval in form and cannot readily be completely occluded by a round body; moreover, in the heart, in such a condition, there is no arrangement as in a ball-valve, by which the ball, should it once chance to roll into the orifice, may be held there, and so it cannot the next moment be thrown out.

He can see no reason, if the conditions during life were as found at autopsy, in the case of Macleod, why the clot should not have passed on into the pulmonary artery. He excludes it altogether from this class of thrombi, and believes that it was most probably made loose on opening the heart post mortem. He further states that the two cases mentioned by him were seen at least once each day "by most competent clinical observers," but in neither of the cases was any symptom observed that could be referred from their suddenness back to an occlusion of the narrowed orifice by the ball-thrombus.

He is firm in his conviction that no greater pathological significance can be attributed to them than to "those ball-thrombi or phleboliths arising in the lumen of vessels, varices, and cylindrical dilatations of veins."

In 1885 Hertz,* in a paper on the formation of cardiac thrombi, takes up the discussion of movable ball-thrombi and reports two additional cases. He believes them to be formed by a portion of an old thrombus in the heart cavity breaking loose and, instead of passing on out of the heart as an embolus, becoming lodged in one of the cavities by meeting with an orifice that is too small for it to pass through. Out of the literature accessible to him he was able to find only the one case of Macleod, a remark on which v. Recklinghausen subsequently criticises him in a review of his paper, because v. Recklinghausen's observations had not been mentioned. His cases are briefly as follows:

First case (Engle-Reimers), a man, 23 years of age, a journeyman tailor, who had as a child suffered from acute joint rheumatism and

* *Loc. cit.*

had suffered for a long time with palpitation of the heart and dyspnœa. After a short stay in the hospital he improved and went out of his own accord. However, he soon had a recurrence of his cardiac incompetency and had to return to the hospital.

At the time of the second admission he had a moderately good appearance, pale cyanotic face, marked edema of the lower extremities, slight ascites. The heart appeared dilated both to the right and to the left. The point of maximal impulse was in the sixth interspace and at the same point there was a distinctly palpable thrill. The heart was irregular in action and gave over the apex a loud systolic and diastolic murmur which diminished in intensity on passing upward. The second pulmonic was distinctly accentuated. The liver border was two finger breadths below the costal margin. The urine contained albumin, was diminished in quantity, specific gravity 1018. By the use of digitalis the patient's condition improved, apparently; the heart's action became more regular, its dullness diminished, and diuresis increased. Later a femoral embolus appeared and finally gangrene of the foot developed. After having been in the hospital a little over a month there was complaint of nausea, but no vomiting. Toward evening of the same day there was an apparently rapid increase of the heart's action and of dyspnœa; cold sweats and cold extremities persisted till morning, when death followed.

Clinical Diagnosis.—Insufficiency and stenosis of the mitral valve, embolism of the right femoral artery, thrombosis of the left auricle.

At section the following conditions were noted. Dry gangrene of the right heel, embolism of the femoral and posterior tibial arteries, occlusion of the vena profunda femoris and thigh veins by old thrombi, left-sided pleurisy with effusion. The heart was markedly dilated in all its chambers, and both ventricles were markedly hypertrophied; there was atheromatous degeneration of the pulmonary artery, and the tricuspid leaflets were thickened and wrinkled. "The left auricle is dilated, the appendix thrombosed, and contains two large thrombus masses. Of these one is globular in shape with an irregular base, still fastened to the auricular appendix by a pedicle; the other is perfectly round, and is free in the auricular cavity. (Figure 2.) This last one has on its surface numerous depressions, apparently as if nibbled out; a single one of which communicates with a central softening on the inside of the thrombus mass." This thrombus measures about 2.5 centimeters in diameter. The surface, except for the defect mentioned,

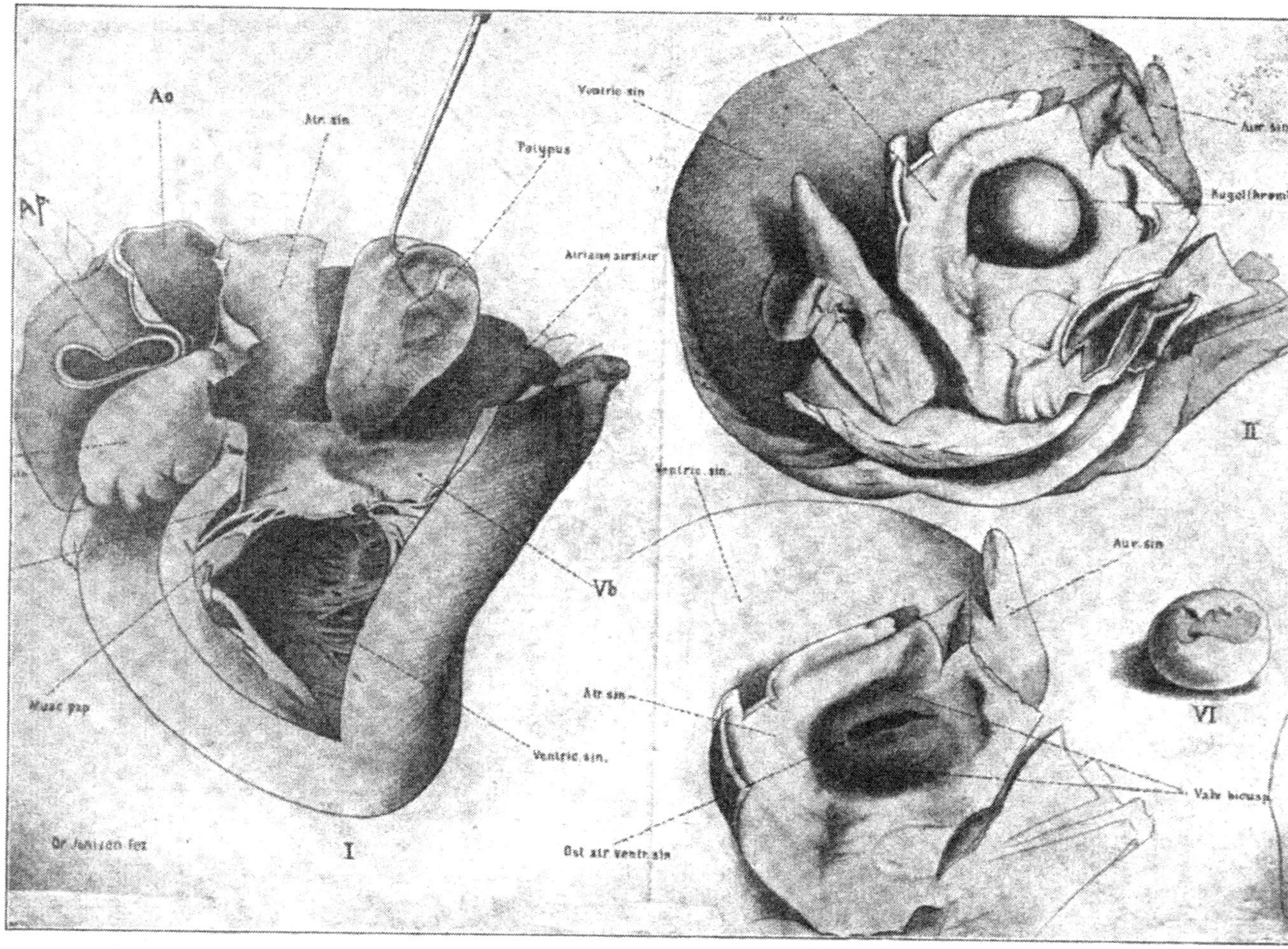

Fig. 2.—Hertz's First Case.

I. Pedunculated heart polyp (Case 1). The left heart is opened from the side, the polyp with a hook is drawn up. *Ao* = aorta, *Ap* = Arteria pulmonalis, *Vb* = Bicuspid valve.

II. Free ball-thombus (Case 1). Left atrium is opened from the side and above, the wall laid open. The ball-thrombus rested in the funnel formed by the stenosis of the valvula mitralis, and covered as a ball-valve the ostium venosum sinistrum.

III. The left auricle in the same situation drawn after the removal of the ball-thrombus.

VI. The ball-thrombus (natural size).

appears "as if fastened on a lathe and polished smooth. The inside is occupied by an irregular cavity, the walls of which are formed by a very brittle thrombus mass. . . . .

"The mitral orifice is markedly stenosed and so narrowed that one cannot get the tip of the little finger through it. Its border is beset with small coxcomb-like excrescences. Both flaps of the valve are along their free border completely fused with each other and form an apparently deep, in its lower half, rigid funnel.. . . . . The chordæ tendineæ are thickened, greatly shortened; the papillary muscles markedly developed." The aorta was narrowed and thin walled; infarcts were present in both lungs and spleen; there was a nutmeg liver, and the kidneys were scarred and fibrous. He refers to his pictures to demonstrate how the thrombus might have closed the orifice of this mitral valve "after the manner of a ball-valve."

His second case (Hansen) was a patient, sex not stated, 39 years old, affected with mania, who had suffered for years with a weak heart, diagnosed mitral stenosis and insufficiency. The patiend died suddenly after symptoms of hydrops had occurred.

On section considerable effusion was found in both pleural cavities; the heart was markedly dilated, and the right ventricle hypertrophied, containing no fibrin clots other than a ball-thrombus which was present in the left auricle and rolled out when the pulmonary veins were cut across, in removing the heart. The ball was round and measured four centimeters in diameter. It had a fibrinous compact integument, two to three millimeters thick and contained in its center a turbid, yellowish-colored fluid mixed with flakes of fibrin. At one point it showed a roughened surface, as if it had "lain on the wall of the auricle or grown upon it" at this point. The mitral orifice was contracted to an opening smaller than the tip of the little finger; both the valve flaps were drawn together and thickened.

He then gives a summary of Macleod's case. Hereupon Hertz enters into a discussion of the pathology of these ball-thrombi. His first case furnishes him with the best evidence for his theory. that the rounding and smoothing of the surface of the ball had been accomplished by a process analogous to the smoothing of the pebbles on the seashore by the washing of the waves; that is, there was a grinding off of the corners and prominences of the clot by a rubbing of its surface against the wall of the auricle and the excrescences on the mitral valve. Moreover, these rubbed-off pieces were borne along in the blood stream and gave rise to the infarcts in the lungs and spleen, and the emboli in the femoral artery. The defect on the surface of the ball was most probably due to a stab by one of the valve excrescenses, he thinks. He notes the absence of any disease of the tricuspid valve in Macleod's case, but believes that the thrombus must have been formed by enormous "weakening which the heart's action during the several attacks of cholera must have suffered." He also mentions the absence of infarcts in this and his last case, but offers no explanation. His first case, he argues, furnishes a convincing proof for the origin of these thrombi from heart polypi.

In his discussion of the clinical symptoms he follows closely Macleod's case and evidently believes the thrombus produced a sudden cessation of the circulation, a point which v. Recklinghausen subsequently contested. He repeats the view promulgated by J. Wickham Legg several years before that the thrombus may act as a ball-valve. This, at first, probably by a weakening of the blood stream, enabled it to roll out of its position over the valve; afterwards, in consequence of regained strength of the heart's action, or from some unknown cause, it was again thrown into the valve orifice, with a repetition of the symptoms, convulsion, loss of consciousness, etc., which this time resulted in the death of the patient. However, the fact that death did not follow suddenly, the patient remaining alive almost two days after the first attack, shows conclusively, he believes, that the occlusion of the orifice was not complete. He notes the correspondence in the symptoms between this case and that of pulmonary embolism. He argues that the symptoms in Macleod's case were those due solely to the ball-thrombus, while in the other two cases which he reports, there was the complication of a mitral stenosis and insufficiency, and no symptoms were noted that are not commonly met with in connection with these affections.

In 1886 T. Lang[11] in Wien, writing on "The Clinical Symptoms of Free Ball-Thrombi of the Heart," on the basis of the cases of this affection reported by Hertz and v. Recklinghausen, notes the difference and coincidence of their views. He is evidently more in sympathy with the views of Hertz and takes for his principal thesis why a freely movable ball-thrombus can remain enclosed in an auricle without giving rise to severe and more characteristic symptoms than any of the cases reported had shown. In opposition to the views of v. Recklinghausen he believes the ball-thrombus can act as a ball-valve and can produce certain symptoms and that, in spite of the fact that the funnel-shaped mitral valve may be oval and the ball-thrombus round, the thrombus is elastic and more or less soft, so that if it were once caught in the orifice, sufficient pressure from above, if the valve orifice were rigid, would cause it to be moulded to the shape of the orifice and thus produce complete occlusion of the valve. Moreover, the motion of blood in the auricle and any body that may be in it during the contraction of the auricle must follow the general laws of hydraulics: accordingly, no particular arrangement for catching or holding the ball, as v. Recklinghausen intimates, is necessary. The reason the ball is not held in the orifice and that these patients can live so long in such a condition is, he believes, because the horizontal pressure necessary to hold the ball in this position is used up in overcoming the resistance presented by the stiffened mitral orifice, by its stenosis, by the great amount of friction, and, finally, by the fact that some of the muscles producing the horizontal pressure are attached to the stiffened or rigid orifice. A part of the free contents of the auricle, inclusive of the ball-thrombus, must consequently remain behind in the auricle. Still he is not willing to exclude the possibility that finally by some movement, which may not proceed from the auricular contraction, the ball may roll on the valve orifice, be pressed into it, and cause a complete interruption of the circulation.

In 1890 William Osler [12] reported from the Montreal General Hospital a case of "Large ball-thrombus, free in left auricle; mitral stenosis."

"Female, age 35, who had for twenty years been subject to attacks of shortness of breath, which had become worse within the past three years. Two years ago she had an attack of acute rheumatism, and during the past eight years she had an attack of right-sided hemiplegia, with aphasia. Speech returned in a few days, but the hemiplegia persisted for some months. Within a year she had a second attack, since which time the paralysis has persisted. When admitted there was orthopnea; face suffused; no dropsy; complete hemiplegia; the heart's action was very irregular; pulse 112, rapid and feeble; the cardiac dullness was increased; the apex beat in normal situation. There was a blowing systolic murmur in the mitral region. Temperature 101° F. Urine contained 50 per cent of albumin. The patient became rapidly worse, cyanosis increased, and death followed five days after admission.

"*Autopsy.*—Well nourished woman. . . . . Heart large, distended with blood clots. . . . . The left auricle was greatly enlarged, and contained fluid blood and clots. Among these was a ball-thrombus, ovoid in shape, the size of a small pullet egg, measuring 3.5 by 2.5 centimeters. It was quite unattached and lay free above the mitral orifice. It was firm and elastic to the touch, and on the surface greyish brown in color, and presented a little linear fibrinous elevation, but no rough spot, as if it had been adherent to the wall. It gave an indistinct sense of fluctuating as if central softening had occurred. . . . . There were no mural thrombi in the chamber. . . . . The right chambers were greatly dilated. The auricular face of the tricuspid valve presented fresh vegetations, many of them pedunculated. The walls of the ventricle were greatly thickened. The mitral orifice was very narrow, just admitting the tip of the little finger; from the auricle it looked like a little buttonhole. At the bottom there was a funnel-shaped depression. The edges of the orifice were thick, of cartilaginous consistence, and were fringed with small vegetations. The chordæ tendineæ were short, particularly those from the anterior muscle, which was attached almost directly upon the flap. The left ventricle was small. The aortic valves were opaque and presented rows of vegetations. There was chronic congestion of lungs and spleen. No fresh infarcts. Right kidney showed several old healed scars."

He then reviews briefly Hertz's and Macleod's cases, and refers to v. Recklinghausen's statement as to his reporting the first case. He also, apparently, had overlooked Wood's, Ogle's and Legg's cases. He agrees with v. Recklinhausen that these ball-thrombi are "globular thrombi detached from the auricular appendix. . . . . It is not likely that these produce any special symptoms."

In 1890 J. Arnold[13] wrote an article concerning "The Occurrence and Consequence of Free Ball-Thrombi of the Heart." He is the first of the German authors to commit the error of giving v. Recklinghausen the credit of first describing this condition. He mentions Macleod's supposed case and the cases reported by Hertz. He notes the coincidence of the opinions of v. Recklinghausen and Hertz as to the formation of these balls "by the loosening of a former mural thrombus, and the divergence of their ideas concerning the manner of the rounding off of this detached thrombus and also the debated question as to whether it could act as a ball-valve and suddenly and completely occlude the stenosed orifice of the mitral valve, and the appearance and character of subsequent symptoms. He reviews Lang's discussion on the subject, notes the rare occurrence of these thrombi and the necessity for further observation to clear up the debated points concerning them, and thereupon reports from the clinic of Erb the following case:

A maid servant who had pneumonia five years before with no subsequent complication, no history of rheumatism or heart trouble, ten days before entering the hospital caught cold; two days later, palpitation of the heart and oppression in the chest were noted; two days later bloody colored mucus was coughed up and severe pains in the back followed.

Physical examination showed a slight cyanosis of skin of face and lips; edema of legs; normal respiration; diastolic and systolic thrill over area of maximal impulse; marked increased area of heart dullness; piping râles over the chest; a prediastolic rough murmur becoming louder and more distinct in diastole over the heart apex, indistinct diastolic murmur over the tricuspid area as well as over the aortic and pulmonary areas; second pulmonic accentuated, heart's action irregular, sometimes intermittent; splenic dullness increased; urine, acid reaction, turbid, specific gravity 1026, containing considerable albumin, a few hyaline and granular casts, many red blood cells; pulse small, soft, easily suppressed and sometimes intermittent.

Clinical Diagnosis.—Malignant endocarditis, general edema (ascites, anasarca), hypostatic pneumonia in the lower lobes of both lungs, parenchymatous nephritis, liver and spleen tumor.

Seven days after admission severe orthopnea and distress began; pulse very small, expectoration bloody and abundant, cyanosis increased, systolic murmur very distinct. Six days later there was an exacerbation of the distress and cyanosis, and the edema became so severe as to burst.

Four weeks after admission with increased distress and cyanosis the patient died.

The autopsy showed cyanosis of face, edema of extremities, face and abdomen, development and nutrition good, skeleton strong, heart free, pericardial cavity filled with clear yellow fluid, injection and ecchymosis in the pericardium.

The heart was enlarged especially as to both the auricles and the right ventricle. "In the right heart, fluid blood and fresh dark clots. In the left atrium fluid blood: on opening it one sees lying on the markedly contracted mitral orifice, a freely movable ball mass, the diameter of which is about 3.2 cm., which weighs about 9.55 grams. Its surface is in general free and symmetrical, grey-yellowish-red color; on a round place, measuring 8 mm. the superficial layer appears broken, and the ball has a knobby, somewhat spotted, surface, yet these are quite flat and completely polished; 7 mm. from the margin of this place there is a short thin filiform process (Fig. 3). By touching the ball one feels that it contains a fluid mass and the peripheral strata is very thin." The endocardium of the left auricle appeared normal. The left auricular appendix was filled with a "greyish-red clot" which was soft in the center and extended as far as the opening into the atrium and ended in "rounded off points. . . . . .

FIG. 3.—ARNOLD'S CASE.
Ball-thrombus out of the left auricle; in the middle an 8 mm. sized, round place, with which it probably lay on the orifice of the auricular appendix; on the right a narrow band-like process. Natural size.

"The mitral valve has a long oval form, measures in one direction 8 mm., in the other 6 mm. The valve flaps grown together and thickened form a firm membrane. The greatly thickened and markedly shortened chordæ tendineæ are fastened behind the line of closure." The musculature of the right ventricle was considerably thickened; that of the left ventricle, less thickened.

There were left pleural adhesions, and the thoracic cavity contained a quantity of reddish colored serum. The right pleural cavity contained gas and bloody-colored fluid and particles of fibrin; the pleura was covered partly with a thick layer of fibrin and showed a necrotic area the size of a nut. Infarcts were present in both lobes, fresh and old, one of which had undergone purulent transformation. The pulmonary artery in its large branches showed no clots.

The abdominal cavity contained a quantity of serous fluid; the spleen was enlarged and firm, of dark red color; kidneys small, enormously congested, in places contracted, capsule held firmly. The mucous membrane of the intestines and stomach was dark red and showed numerous hemorrhages; the aorta was thin walled and narrow.

"*Anatomical Diagnosis.*—Chronic endocarditis. Stenosis of the mitral valve and insufficiency. Ball-thrombus in the left atrium and adherent thrombi in the left auricular appendix. Dilation of the left auricle and right heart, relative insufficiency of the tricuspid valve. Multiple infarcts in both lungs. Necrosis and perforation of right pleura. Right pneumothorax, right sero-fibrinous pleurisy. Chronic venous hyperæmia. Chronic nephritis and insufficiency of the kidneys."

He then discusses his case, comparing its points of resemblance to and its differences from the cases reported by v. Recklinghausen and Hertz. He believes that in his case, the ball-thrombus had been formed by a loosening of a portion of the clot formed in the left auricular appendix when it had been attached either by fine threads, or over the whole area, for a period, at the round knobby place on the surface of the ball, which was about the size of the opening of the appendix into the atrium. He is not absolutely sure the thrombus had not been torn loose by manipulation of the heart at autopsy, nor is he sure whether the rounding and polishing of the surface of the ball took place while it was attached or after it became loosened and free.

As to the formation of the thrombus, as well as its subsequent loosening, he is sure the chronic endocarditis and mitral stenosis played a great part. The consequent congestion and stagnation of the blood in the left auricle, he believes, was sufficient to explain the presence of the thrombus and the stenosis of the mitral valve its retention in the cavity of the auricle.

As to whether a free ball-thrombus will or can produce, during life, any severe symptoms, he was not able to say definitely from the symptoms of his case. The marked cardiac disturbance which occurred three weeks before the death of his patient might have been produced by a transitory occlusion of the mitral valve, but the presence of the numerous infarcts in the lungs would explain the symptoms as well. That the ball was not pressed into the mitral orifice as it would have to be (as he accepts the views of v. Recklinghausen) to produce severe symptoms, is evidenced by the fact that it was not broken, and that it was so soft in the center that such pressure must necessarily have broken it.

He is not willing to confirm or deny Lang's opinion, but accepts it as a possibility that the ball, by some process, "rolls on" the orifice and temporarily obstructs the blood current; that the condition for this is most favorable during the diastole of the auricle, he believes, and that by the extreme stenosis of the mitral valve the auricle is not able to empty itself completely and consequently can exercise no horizontal pressure on such a mass as a ball-thrombus.

He concludes that, (1) With a stenosed orifice an occlusion by a ball-thrombus does not necessarily have to follow; (2) Up to that time no observations had been afforded to show that under these circumstances such an occlusion can follow; (3) When an occlusion, in general, is possible, it is brought about not by a horizontal pressure on the ball-thrombus, but by the thrombus rolling itself over or on the orifice, probably at the time of systole of the ventricle; (4) That a freely movable ball-thrombus can form and be retained in the auricle for a long time and with a normal orifice is yet to be proven.

In 1890 Fürbringer[*] demonstrated to the Medical Society of Berlin a heart obtained from a child that had died of scarlet fever, with symptoms of uremia and signs of sudden heart failure. The specimen showed about 15 pea-to-cherry sized, and even smaller, thrombi, which, partly free, partly mechanically held fast like clay-ticks to the skin, were seated on the musculi pectinati, of the right auricle. "No trace of mitral stenosis was present."

These were evidently not ball-thrombi and show, as noted by Welch,* that he had not the correct conception of the true nature of these bodies.

In 1890, also, Von Ziemssen[*] gave an account of one case of ball-thrombus along with a presentation of two cases of polypoid thrombi. He gives v. Recklinghausen the credit for reporting the first cases of ball-thrombi, mentions his cases, the so-called case of Macleod and the two cases described by Hertz. He discourses on ball-thrombi in general, following v. Recklinghausen very closely as to their origin and subsequent growth. In his case the old thrombus nucleus was easily distinguished on cross section as well as by the fine laminated covering. On the surface there were numerous small cup-like depressions and from each depression, on cross section, there was a fine cord passing to the central nucleus. These strands were distinctly older than the new

* *Loc. cit.*

laminæ, and he believed the small depressions were produced "by organization and contraction of these strands."

The clinical picture of ball-thrombi he declares the same as that of large pedunculated thrombi. He believes, from an analysis of his cases and those reported in the literature, that a probable diagnosis of autochthonous thrombosis (by which he means ball-thrombi and pedunculated thrombi) is possible under the following conditions: (1) the physical proof of a mitral stenosis; (2) the appearance of a severe obstruction to the current in the left heart (cyanosis, dyspnœa, coldness of the extremities, etc.) in a more marked degree than in mitral stenosis. He further mentions a symptom that was present in all three of his cases and in one of the cases reported by Hertz, viz., circumscribed gangrene in the feet with edema and cadaveric coldness and, especially in his cases, an obliteration of the arterial pulse of the lower extremities. He believes the gangrene might be due to an occlusion of the vessels not alone by emboli but also by arterial thrombi consequent upon the diminished peripheral blood supply.

In 1891 zum Busch[16] in his inaugural dissertation, at the Albert-Ludwigs University at Freiburg, "On the Construction of Heart Thrombi and Their Relation to the Heart Wall," argued that the disturbance in the circulation was the principal factor and that the change in the endocardium and musculature were of no consideration in the formation of heart thrombi. Following the classification of Hertz for these bodies, he briefly comments on seven cases of ball-thrombi collected "from the literature accessible to him." He gives v. Recklinghausen the honor of describing the first case and mentions besides the cases of Hertz, Macleod, v. Ziemssen and Arnold, and the controversy between the views of Hertz and v. Recklinghausen and Arnold, as to whether these thrombi may temporarily or permanently obstruct the circulation with the consequent manifestation of recognizable and distinctive symptoms.

In 1892 Schorl[17] demonstrated before the Medical Society of Leipzig a heart with marked mitral stenosis, in the left auricle of which a free ball-thrombus of the size of a hen's egg was found. Its surface was for the most part smooth, but at one point showed a rounded process. The left auricular appendix was filled with a thrombus which projected into the atrium of the auricle. He refers to the views of v. Recklinghausen and Arnold as to the mode of origin of these thrombi, and states that no clinical symptoms were demonstrated in his case.

In the discussion Curschmann stated that he had seen these ball-thrombi three times and in all three cases mitral stenosis existed and death came suddenly. There is doubt among some of the authors as to whether this is not the same case as reported by Krumholz. It is also nowhere stated, that I know of, whether this is the same case as shown in his *Stereo-scopische-photographisher Atlas* (Fig. 4) or not. However, from the above description and that accompanying his picture, I judge that it is.

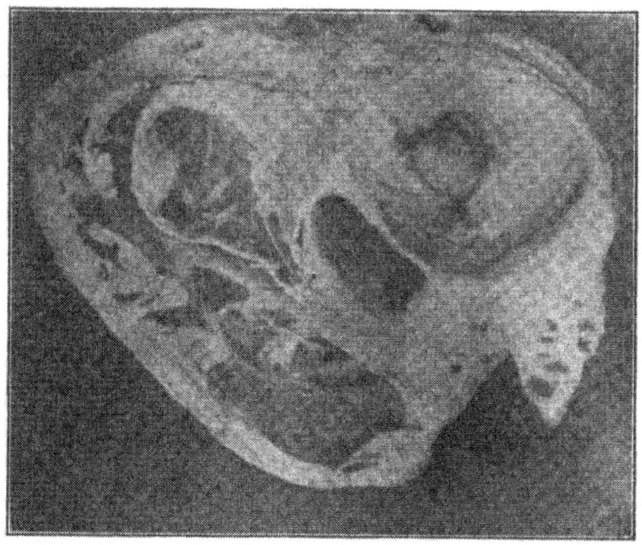

Fig. 4.—Schmorl's Case.

In 1892 Redtenbacher[18] described "A Case of a Pedunculated and a Ball-Thrombus in the Left Auricle." He reviews v. Ziemssen's cases as reported at Vienna to the 9th Congress for Internal Medicine and notes that what v. Ziemssen's cases showed in separate hearts, his showed in the same heart. He then mentions v. Ziemssen's grouping of symptoms for a probable diagnosis of autochthonous thrombi and describes the following case:

A female manual laborer, 46 years of age, who was seen by him only once after admission to the hospital, in which she remained about 48 hours before death, had had scarlet fever 10 years before and rheumatism five years before admission. The rheumatism recurred after one year and was accompanied by marked palpitation of the heart and great distress. Since then she had suffered continually with palpitation of the heart and was unable to work, coming into the hospital because of increased cardiac distress.

Physical examination showed a sparely built, markedly emaciated woman, skin pale, marked edema of feet, lower extremities of a pale and livid color, smooth, shiny, and very tense; temperature markedly lowered and of death-like coldness to the touch; radial pulse scarcely palpable; heart dullness increased on both sides, a marked thrill on palpation, a distinct pre-systolic and systolic murmur over the apex on ausculation; second pulmonic strongly accentuated; liver swollen.

Diagnosis.—Extreme mitral stenosis with broken compensation, hypertrophy of the heart, possibly aortic stenosis.

Autopsy.—Marked edema and pallor of the extremities. Brain and meninges normal. The right pleural cavity contained half a liter of serum, lung free; left lung free in front, adherent behind, cavity contained quarter of a liter of bloody fluid; pleuræ covered with fibrinous hemorrhagic exudate; both lungs rusty brown in color, somewhat emphysematous and dry, pigmented; infarct in left lower lobe. Pericardium markedly dilated, contained some serum; heart enlarged three-fold, especially the right half; the right auricle taking up two-thirds of the heart's surface, hence the left ventricle appeared smaller than normal; left ventricle contained fluid blood; its wall 0.5 cm. thick, its endocardium delicate and thin; mitral valve contracted to size of tip of little finger, buttonhole shape, margins grown together, presenting a thick, shrunken, short, solid funnel; chordæ tendineæ grown together and contracted. The left auricle is enlarged to the size of one's fist and contains besides fluid blood a ball-thrombus having a diameter of 3.5 cm. This ball is round, soft, easily fluctuating. Its surface is smooth, brownish red, studded with the finest grey fibrinous threads. In the left auricular appendix, projecting into the auricular cavity, there is a thrombus fastened by a long pedicle. The endocardium is slightly thickened and dull. The bicuspid orifice was narrowed by adhesions and thickening of the valve edges to the size of one's finger; chordæ tendineæ thickened and contracted; endocardium slightly dulled and thickened; aortic cusps thin on their borders, otherwise slightly thickened; aorta somewhat narrowed and thin walled; pulmonary artery broad, cusps thin, intima here and there slightly thickened; heart muscle dark, dirty red color, very firm; marked passive congestion of liver, spleen and kidneys; cyanotic atrophy of liver; infarcts in lower pole of left kidney; chronic metritis, endometritis and colpitis; congestive catarrah of stomach and intestines.

He excuses himself for not making a diagnosis of the ball-thrombus, according to v. Ziemssen's symptom complex, by the fact that he was able to observe the case for such a short period and that the symptom of circumscribed gangrene had not developed. He believes there was a genetic relation between the pedunculated thrombus in his case and the ball-thrombus, that the ball-thrombus was at one time a "whip-shaped auricular thrombus," which developed during a period when the mitral orifice was contracted to a marked degree. It subsequently broke loose; it then lost its whip shape, could not pass the contracted orifice and by rotation and the application of fibrin, became a smooth surfaced ball-thrombus.

In 1892 T. Lang[19] reported the case of a 44 year old female who was observed while subject to attacks of severe tachicardia, coming on suddenly and without warning, and associated with fits of weakness and fainting spells. These attacks he considers due to a partial obstruction of the stenosed mitral valve and the greater part of his paper is devoted to a discussion of how and why a freely movable ball-thrombus may partially and completely for a time obstruct the circulation. He mentions v. Recklinghausen's views on this point and the cases of Hertz and v. Ziemssen. He gives no account of a post mortem examination of his case and his diagnosis must, of course, be considered very doubtful.

Rosenbach[20] in his book on "Diseases of the Heart," published in 1893, in his article on thrombosis of the heart, discusses briefly, with respect more to the clinical picture, ball-thrombi. He mentions the views of Hertz v. Recklinghausen, and v. Ziemssen and gives very briefly a case that had come under his observation. In this case there was mitral stenosis with formation of a nut-size ball-thrombus in the left auricle. Clinically there was a remarkably loud presystolic and diastolic murmur in the 2d and 3d intercostal spaces near the left sternal border, but with no whirr of mitral insufficiency at the apex.

The localization of the whirr, he believes, might be turned to account, if the possibility of an anomaly of the pulmonary orifice could be excluded.

Krumbholz,[a] writing in 1893 "Upon the Causation of Pedunculated and Ball-Thrombi," refers to the papers of v. Recklinghausen, v. Ziemssen and Hertz and gives briefly the clinical histories and autopsy findings of two additional cases.

His first case was that of a seamstress 41 years of age, who came to the hospital because of attacks, in the last week, of shortness of breath and palpitation of the heart, from which she had suffered for some time before. Twelve years before she had had for three weeks joint rheumatism, and since then the attacks had occurred repeatedly, but disappeared under medical attention.

Physical examination showed the general signs of a mitral stenosis and insufficiency, with some undetermined affection of the aortic valve. After about five weeks stay in the hospital she was well enough to be dismissed. A week later, however, she returned with the same general signs and symptoms; albumin in the urine was noted at this time. After remaining in the hospital about a month she went out, only to return again about six weeks later, when she came in for the third time. On this admission it was noted that she was very cyanotic and the dyspnœa and irregularity of the heart's action were considerable. The lower extremities were cold and edematous. A week later she died.

Post Mortem Examination.—Pericardial cavity contained about 30 cc. of serous fluid; heart enlarged. "On opening the left auricle a ball-thrombus of the form and size of a hen's egg, apparently of firm consistency and everywhere of smooth surface, is easily removed from it. On one pole is a perceptible spot on which it apparently stood, together with an attached thrombus that completely filled the auricular appendix"; mitral valve flaps thickened into a stiff narrow ring, papillary muscles hypertrophied, tendons shortened and thickened; aortic cusps, in general, thin; on the right anterior and posterior cusps there was slight thickening which prevented complete closure; right auricle dilated; the wall of right ventricle not thickened. "By subsequent examination * it appeared that the thrombus possessed an endothelial covering and had a lamellar structure." He believes there was no symptom manifest that could not have been explained by the condition found to have existed in the heart.

He then reports a case of polypoid thrombosis of the right auricle and says that also in this case there was on microscopical examination "an endothelial covering" to this thrombus.

* Supposedly microscopical.

In 1893 Stange[22] reported from Ebstein's clinic "A Case of Ball-Thrombus in the Auricle of the Left Heart," autopsied by Orth.

He reviews the literature, and credits v. Recklinghausen with giving the name "ball-thrombus" to this class of bodies. He mentions the cases reported by Hertz, Arnold, Osler, and Krumbholz. He then presents in great detail another case which may be summarized as follows:

A male teacher, 21 years of age, was admitted to the hospital complaining that he had been suffering for five weeks with palpitation of the heart which was especially manifest after exertion and excitement. Previous history: repeated attacks of pain in stomach moving toward left shoulder; influenza one year before of eight days' duration; articular rheumatism in lower thigh with swelling, about three months before. Physical examination: medium nourished, lies on back by preference, skin of face and hands flushed and cyanotic; rapid pulse, 116; no edema; bowing of precordial region of chest; expanding pulsation between the 5th and 6th ribs inside the mammillary line; systolic thrill plainest at apex; heart more markedly dilated towards the left; pre-systolic murmur over the apex; second sound indistinct; second pulmonic accentuated; over the left auricle a systolic murmur and a loud accentuated second sound; over the pulmonary and aortic areas a systolic and diastolic murmur, also over the tricuspid valve and abdominal aorta; râles in lower posterior left lung; liver and spleen enlarged; urine contained albumin and casts; spine curved forward.

Clinical Diagnosis.—Insufficiency of myocardium . . . . ., aortic insufficiency, nephritis.

In the hospital, with rest in bed and tincture of valerian, the patient at first improved. However, about four weeks after admission, palpitation of the heart returned with pain and air hunger. This condition, in the course of a few days, was aggravated by a steadily diminishing quantity of urine and increase of albumin, by pain in stomach and vomiting, pallor, slight icterus, edema of joints, coughing and spitting up of blood. He was found dead in bed after having been known to have arisen one hour before. He was in the hospital about five weeks.

Autopsy.—The heart appeared double pointed. The long dimension seemed less increased than the width; both ventricles were dilated; right auricle markedly, the left auricle less dilated. Inside the left ventricle there was a walnut-sized thrombus that had existed free in the auricle (Fig. 5). It had a convex-ribbed surface, of dirty red color, which was marked by numerous projecting ridges, appearing as grey elevations; the other more flattened surface was slightly ribbed, and had in its center an opening out of which a papillary projection extended, giving the whole mass very much the appearance of a fungoid growth. Nowhere on the entire surface was a torn place apparent. On section it was of a grey red color through which ran numerous fine and coarse greyish red strands which took their origin from the papilla-like projection and radiated from it, fan-wise, to the surface where they projected as ridges. The thrombus was everywhere rather firm in consistency, nowhere any softening to be seen or felt. The heart muscle was thickened over the right conus, over the apex thinned

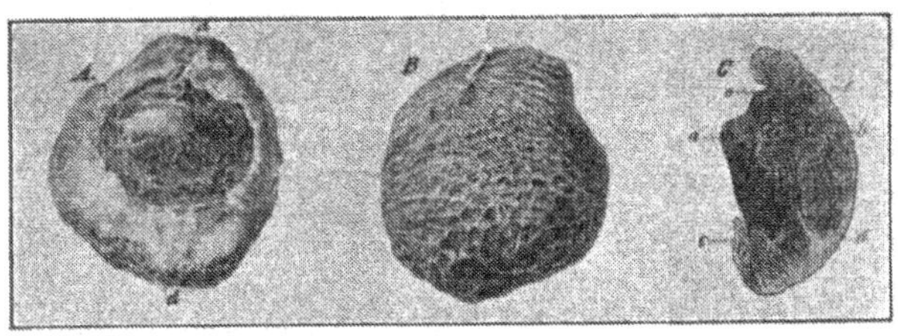

FIG. 5.—P. STANGE'S CASE.

A and B, the two flat surfaces of the thrombus in natural size. C, cross section in natural size of A from d to d.

to 1 mm. It was of a light brown color, flecked with yellow, especially marked in the papillary muscles. The wall of the left auricle and appendix was thickened. In between the muscle bands of the appendix there was a bean-sized, greyish thrombus, the surface of which was everywhere smooth. The tricuspid valve was practically normal in width, the flaps only along their anterior borders were a little thickened.

Anatomical Diagnosis.—Aortic endocarditis with fusion of valve cusps; retraction of the septum with marked thickening, in places calcification; destruction of the posterior valve cusps; aneurism of the sinus of the left cusp; marked dilatation with slight hypertrophy of the left ventricle; shortening of the papillary muscle trabeculæ; dilatation of the auricles, somewhat also of the right ventricle; valves fairly normal, congenital fusion of two of the pulmonary cusps; free thrombus in the left auricle, small adherent thrombus on wall of left auricular appendix; fatty degeneration of inner portion of heart muscle; hemorrhagic infarcts and emboli in both lungs; old healing infarcts in both kidneys; congestion in lungs, spleen, kidneys, liver, stomach, and intestines; slight colloid goitre; hypostatic knots in liver; slight fatty change of aortic intima; subpericardial hemorrhage; hydrops of all the serous cavities; edema of the lower extremities.

In the discussion of his case Stange admits that his is not a true ball-thrombus in the sense of v. Recklinghausen; but on the ground that, in this group, all cases of free thrombi in the heart which possess anything like a ball-shape are to be included, he thinks his case can be considered. He notes the unanimous agreement among the authors on the subject that the first essential condition for the formation of these thrombi is a stasis of blood in the heart, produced by muscular weakness or damage of the valve flaps. The thrombus thus originated in the auricular appendix grows out of it into the lumen of the auricle and, after a variable length of time and condition of growth, by some unknown process, breaks loose as a free thrombus.

Considering his own case, he believes that the tip of the papilla of the fungoid thrombus and the point of the smaller thrombus adherent in the auricle were at one time connected, and subsequently became changed by the loosening of the thrombus and the application of new masses of fibrin. He believes that the thrombus might have been free in the auricle about three days, though it had had a much longer comparatively free existence attached only by the papilla-like pedicle. This he considers corroborated by the ribbed surface and the cup-shaped depressions; if it had been free longer it would have been more spherical, reasoning according to v. Recklinghausen. He does not agree with Hertz and his "grinding off" theory for the formation of the smooth surface. The absence of softening or regressive change in the center of the thrombus he considers another point in favor of his view that the thrombus had existed only a short time free in the auricle. He compares the fine and coarse grey cords observed on section of his thrombus with those observed in v. Ziemssen's case and notes the marked difference. He believes with Zchu [23] and Aschoff [24] that these represented collections of blood platelets and the ribs were ends of blood platelet strands. He notes the difference in the condition of the mitral valve found in his case from that in most of the cases reported in the literature, but offers no explanation for it.

As to the symptomatology, he discusses at length the view held by Hertz and Lang, that such a thrombus may produce severe symptoms and even sudden death, and the opposing one of v. Recklinghausen that such a thrombus in itself may give rise to no special and characteristic symptoms. He agrees with Hertz and believes the sudden onset of marked pallor in his case, observed about three days before death, was the indication of the separation of the pedunculated thrombus and an obstruction of the circulation through the mitral orifice. He does not believe that any great diagnostic importance can be attached to v. Ziemssen's symptom of circumscribed gangrene.

In conclusion Stange states that while ball-thrombi are most commonly found in the left auricle, associated with diseased conditions of the mitral orifice, they may also be found with a comparatively normal mitral valve if their diameter is so large that they cannot pass the orifice; that they can conform themselves to the orifice, thus bringing about a temporary closure of it and severe symptoms, or complete occlusion, and sudden death. He believes that the occurrence of v. Ziemssen's syndrom is exceedingly rare.

In 1895 Bostroem,[a] writing from the Pathological Institute at Giessen "Concerning Thrombus-like Formations in the Heart," described a very old specimen he found in the museum at that place (Fig. 6). He could learn nothing of the history of the case, but judged from its size that it belonged to an adult individual; the musculature and valve leaflets were normal. In the right auricle there was fastened to the auricular septum by a very short pedicle an oval body, 5.8 x 5.3 x 5 cm. Its surface was generally smooth and showed no difference from the endocardium, with which the surface of the pedicle was continuous. On the basis of the observations of Choisy, Nuhn, Kottmeier and Prous of the occurrence of primary hemorrhage into the auricular septum, he argues that this case and many of the other cases of reported pedunculated polypi of the heart are nothing other than thrombosed varices. However, he was unable, microscopically, to demonstrate an endothelium and with a probe could find no venous connection. The description of the section of this body when compared with the thrombus in Stange's case is interesting. It was seen to be "made up of fairly uniform fibrinous masses which radiate from the pedicle towards the sides."

His article is briefly reviewed because of his hypothesis that these thrombosed varices of the heart may become detached and form the nuclei of ball-thrombi. In support of this view he refers to the cases of Macleod, Stange and v. Ziemssen.

In 1895 Eichorst,[a] in his "Pathologie und Therapie," under the heading of ball-thrombi mentions that in the preceding six years he had seen three cases at autopsy in his clinic. He gives v. Recklinghausen the credit for describing the first cases and notes that Hertz, Fürbringer, v. Ziemssen and Redtenbacher had described similar cases. He says, "These thrombi are always, perhaps, formed out of loosened parts of mural thrombi, which, aided in a rolling motion by the blood

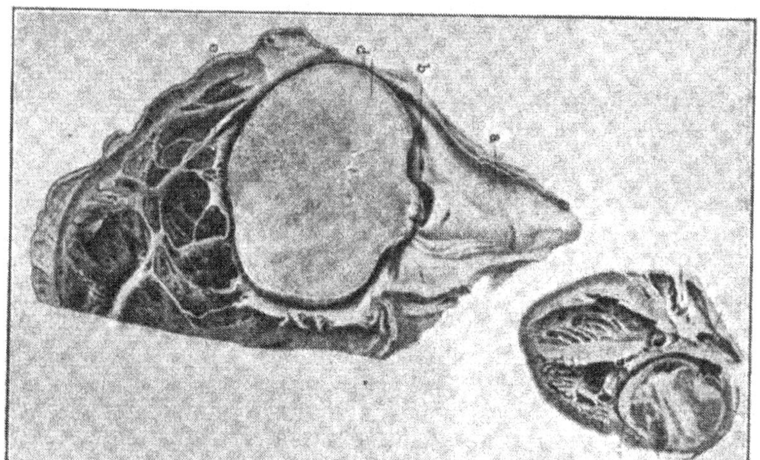

FIG. 6.—E. BOSTROEM'S CASE.

The large body fills the whole right auricle (*a*); the body has drawn out the auricular septum after the manner of a pedicle (*b*), is covered over with a thin (in the drawing all over but on the right drawn too broad) capsular membrane (*d*) which runs into the endocardium of the pedicle and consequently into the endocardium of the auricle and rests upon the lower circumference of the tricuspid valve flaps (*e*).

stream, while in the auricle, obtain a round form, and a lamellar structure by the application of new layers of fibrin, and gradually increase in circumference." He cites v. Ziemssen's grouping of symptoms as an aid in diagnosis.

In 1896 Tauber[n] reported a lengthy case which may be briefly summarized as follows:

An assistant railway manager, 28 years old, had noticed swelling of his ankles for 15 years. A persistent purulent discharge from his nose had been present for eight years. Palpitation of his heart and dyspnœa on exertion had been present for four years. Three months before, the dyspnœa and palpitation became worse and accompanied by such severe edema and pain in the stomach that he sought the hospital.

On admission he was seen to be of middle size, solidly built, somewhat emaciated. The skin was pale and icteric; face and extremities cyanosed, slightly edematous; superficial veins dilated; respiration labored. The apex beat was not evident; systolic retraction in the 5th left interspace. The heart dullness was greatly increased; a systolic murmur of ringing character was heard all over the valve areas; the radial artery soft, pulse arythmic, rate 100; liver markedly swollen, its border rounded; urine turbid with urates, specific gravity 1030, contained bile pigment.

Clinical Diagnosis.—High grade mitral stenosis in the stage of advanced broken compensation.

Therapy.—Infusion of digitalis.

Four days later the temperature was normal, the edema had disappeared, the heart's action was more regular and slower, and the heart and liver were diminished in size. However, vomiting recurred and the digitalis was discontinued. Eight days after admission he vomited bile-stained material; the edema increased, and the liver became larger. This was followed by an increase in the area of the heart's dullness towards the right. Skin hemorrhages developed which increased in size and number till he died.

Autopsy.—Cardiac dilatation. "The left auricle is markedly dilated and filled with solid clots. The mitral orifice admits about the tip of the little finger; its border is ossified, with fine warty excrescences springing from it. Completely free in the auricle, lying loose in the coagula, there is a ball 3.5 cm. in diameter (Fig. 7). Its surface is smooth except at one point. It weighs 25 (?) grams and is seen on cross-section to be made up of concentric layers of grey brown red color, surrounding a boggy mass."

Anatomical Dianosis.—Chronic endocarditis with insufficiency of the bicuspid and tricuspid valves; stenosis of the mitral valve; slight stenosis of the tricuspid valve; dilatation of the right auricle and ventricle; 25 (?) gram thrombus in the left atrium with parietal affection of the endocardium; total adhesion of the pericardium; general venous stasis.

In his discussion Tauber notes a number of the cases reported in the literature and discusses his own case quite thoroughly.

Osler[38] in 1896 reported a case of this affection which was associated with sudden death. He notes the comparatively infrequent occurrence of sudden death in mitral stenosis as compared with aortic valvular disease and then describes the following case.

A young lady, age 20, came into the hospital complaining of swelling of the legs and shortness of breath. Family history not known.

Personal History.—She had diphtheria and scarlet fever 11 years before; for a year or more she had been short of breath on exertion.

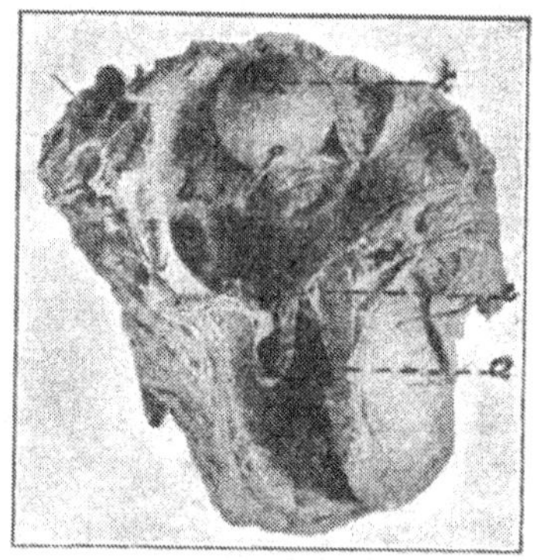

FIG. 7.—E. TAUBER'S CASE.

The left auricle open, *K*, the ball thrombus; *p*, the smooth pole; *e*, the entrance into the auricle; *a*, the stenosed orifice; *b*, the auricular endocardium.

Present Illness.—About two months before she noticed a swelling around her shoe tops which ascended to her hips. This was followed by backache and swelling in the lower portion of the spine. Lately she had had headache and puffiness of the eyes on rising in the morning; appetite poor, bowels irregular.

Physical Examination.—Appeared younger than her real age, well nourished; lips slightly cyanotic, luetic facies—saddle nose, projecting forehead, cloudiness of cornea, central incisor slightly peg-shaped. "Inspection of chest showed a heart impulse in the fourth and fifth interspaces, the maximal in the fifth, 11 cm. from the mid-sternal line. The relative dullness was at the upper border of the third rib. On palpation there was a thrill at the apex, which varied a good deal in intensity. On auscultation, the first sound was very snapping at the apex, and preceded by a rough, harsh, pre-systolic murmur, and there was a soft blowing systolic murmur passing toward the axilla. The first sound had a sharp valvular character. The pre-systolic murmur was lost in the mid-axilla. There was a good deal of echoing over a limited area in the fifth space. In the second and third left intercostal spaces the second sound was very accentuated. The second aortic sound was relatively feeble." Liver enlarged, palpable 6 cm. below the ribs; legs swollen; urine contained a small quantity of albumin and a few hyaline casts.

Under hospital care she improved, the dropsy disappeared, and the heart's action became slower, though she still had a flushed, suffused facies. She was seen the day before death and seemed quite well. She was found by a nurse very cyanotic, gave a gasp or two and died in a few minutes, after remaining in the hospital a little over three weeks.

Post Mortem Examination.—Almost the entire exposed portion of the heart was made up of the right auricle and ventricle, only a small portion of the apex of the left ventricle was apparent; the auricular appendix of the left ventricle not visible. The mitral valve segments were thickened and adherent, the chordæ tendineæ greatly shortened, the orifice just admitting the tip of the index finger; no fresh endocarditis. The left ventricle was relatively small; the right ventricle was very large and hypertrophied. The right auricle was very capacious and relatively thick walled. The left auricle was very large, the endocardium very opaque, and the wall greatly thickened. A ball-thrombus "lies loose in the left auricle, occupying the funnel-shaped space leading to the mitral orifice. It is ovoid, measuring about 3 cm. in length and at one end is roughened, indicating an area of attachment. Beyond the venous engorgement of the viscera there is no other feature of special interest. There are no lesions of congenital syphilis."

Osler believes "that the sudden death in this case was due to the dislodgment of the thrombus and a plugging by it of the narrowed mitral orifice, so that she really died of embolism of the left auriculo-ventricular orifice."

He thereupon cites a case of a three and a half year old child in which a detached sarcomatous thrombus of the left kidney had plugged the tricuspid orifice and a mass the size of a hazelnut the pulmonary orifice. He also mentions the important facts of his former case and enumerates the various forms of thrombi that are found in the heart cavities.

In 1899 Welch * in his article on "Thrombosis and Embolism" for Allbutt's System of Medicine, gave the first and most complete summary of the literature on ball-thrombi that had up to that time been presented. He was the first to give William Wood of Edinburgh the credit for describing the first case and to point out that besides Wood, Ogle and Legg had placed on record cases of this affection several years before the appearance of v. Recklinghausen's book. For a brief statement of the principal facts on ball-thrombi this is undoubtedly the best article in the literature.

In 1900 Löhlein [20] made a complete review of the literature on ball-thrombi and reported an additional case, as follows:

An extremely anemic and decrepit woman, 47 years of age, had a left-sided hemiplegia, and a stenosis and insufficiency of the mitral valve. "Broken compensation existed, which in spite of digitalis and careful attendance did not entirely disappear. There was slight atheroma present; the dependent parts were edematous. The bladder contained a large quantity of urine. The pulse was small, somewhat intermittent. This particular attack had come on suddenly, and was of quite short duration. There had been no similar attacks previously. The patient was seized as she lay quietly in bed, and just as rapidly as the symptoms had appeared, they disappeared. Besides a somewhat marked cyanosis and an enormously rapid pulse, only the anxious expression of the patient, by which the facial paralysis was evidently brought out, in any way indicated the previous injury. On the 29th of August, during a meal, an attack came on to which she succumbed. The woman, who was sitting upright, suddenly sank down, the heart made one more contraction and death ensued. During the eleven days after admission into the hospital, her cyanosis increased steadily."

On section, the heart was found of normal size; the subpericardial fat, especially on the right side, was increased; tendinous patches on the pericardium; right auricle normal; tricuspid valve normal; musculature of right ventricle thickened; pulmonary valve normal. The mitral valve was extremely narrowed, of a buttonhole shape, and quite stiff and rigid; it measured 15 x 5 cm., and was calcified along borders. The left auricle was considerably dilated and its wall thickened

* *Loc. cit.*

to 4 mm.; the endocardium was also thickened; there was a small attached thrombus beneath the fold of the foramen ovale. The left auricular appendix was distended and filled with an old thrombus which projected into the atrium. The lower portion of this thrombus mass was torn and into it there fitted a free clot, very nearly the size and shape of a small walnut. It measured 3.5 x 2.2 x 2.2 cm., was oval, arched on one side and flat on the other. The aortic valve was normal.

He compares at length the symptoms of his case with those of the other cases reported in the literature and finally concludes that, in his case, the thrombus had been loose only a very short time.

In 1901 Wadsworth,[80] of Philadelphia, reported a case to the Philadelphia Pathological Society. He has kindly sent me his notes on this case, and as it has never been published in full, and as he tells me in a personal letter that the report that has been made of it is for the most part wrong, I take this privilege of incorporating his notes in my paper exactly as I have them from him. They are as follows:

J. H., age 40 years, white, male, single. Died April 7, 1901, Philadelphia, Pa.

A stocky medium-sized man, working in an engine factory, had been drinking freely of late, and had laid off work for about a week, probably as a result of his habits. His bed-fellow says "he died about half-past seven, without saying a word."

Making due allowance for the condition of this man the probable account of his death is briefly as follows:

While still fuddled with the liquor taken the night before, which he had been sleeping off quietly, he rolled over on waking and in changing position threw the clot into a new position in the heart and before he was altogether awake his heart stopped beating.

There were no marks of recent violence on the body and no history of anything unusual. Nor was there any history throwing light on the condition which was found.

The lungs were found in extreme congestion, the blood being dark and exuding freely from cut surface, indicating clearly that the right heart had worked strongly against obstruction in the left side.

The heart was greatly distended with dark fluid blood, especially the auricles and vessels leading to them. The muscle was in fair condition. Considerable hypertrophy of left ventricle. Valves of left side show considerable atheroma, but no vegetations. In left auricle a round clot about two inches in diameter, slightly egg-shaped but less than one-half inch difference in diameter. Surface smooth, fairly firm, slightly elastic, but before long became softer and broke, but still the fragments retained the shape of the original. Not homogeneous, one side showed yellowish granular condition.*

I can only say that the ball-clot was clearly of considerable age, not less than a month, and that the organization resembled that found in an aneurism of long standing. About and above the clot was a recent clot in the auricle.

The left auricle was greatly distended by these clots and dark fluid blood; the ball was clearly obstructing the mitral opening, causing practically complete occlusion. I am somewhat puzzled to account for the long life of this man after this had become detached and rounded into its final shape.

There was evidence in the spleen and in the kidneys of old infarcts and it is almost certain that they and the clot had resulted from an old endocarditis which had left scars on the valves of the heart, but which was not active at the time of death.

The organs showed evidence of chronic alcoholism.

The liver was hard, congested and far from normal. The pancreas was firm, mottled and had undergone considerable degeneration. The spleen showed scars, was large and firm. The stomach gave odor of alcohol and showed chronic gastritis, but was nearly empty, in a typical post-alcoholic condition. Intestines as after serious continued alcoholism. Bladder well filled, fairly normal.

Nothing further of note could be found or learned which would throw light on the condition.

(Signed) WILLIAM S. WADSWORTH, M. D.,
Philadelphia, Pa.

Dr. Joseph McFarland[31] has furnished me with the notes of two cases that came under his observation, which he considered cases of ball-thrombi. I also present his notes as received from him. They are as follows:

Philadelphia Hospital, 1900. No. 3126.

J. H. Men's Med. No. 13. Admitted Nov. 28, 1900. Died Dec. 3, 1900.

Primary Diagnosis.—Croupous pneumonia.

History.—J. H. White, age 56, laborer, resident of Philadelphia.

Chief Complaint.—Pain in chest, dyspnœa, weakness, anorexia, loss of weight.

Family History.—Father dead, cause unknown. Mother died of old age. One brother living and well.

Past Medical History.—Small. "Grip" several years ago. Gonorrhea many years ago. Denies syphilis. Uses alcohol and tobacco to some excess.

---

* Notes as to its structure are defective because I had fully expected the person to whom the specimen was delivered to take measurements and to harden the specimen for further study.

Present Illness.—Attack of pleurisy five weeks ago. Dyspnœa, pain in chest, cough, weakness, anorexia, loss of weight.

Condition upon Admission.—Patient emaciated, rather dusky, somewhat delirious. Respiration quick and labored with retraction of the tissues of the neck. Some suppuration in the inner canthus of right eye.

Pupils equal and react to light and accommodation.

Tongue red and dry, and covered with crusts.

Pulse very small, weak and feeble; regular and of low tension. Arteries are atheromatous.

Chest and abdomen greatly emaciated. Expansion diminished particularly on right. Depressions above and below clavicles. Scales over chest.

Heart: Cardiac impulse neither visible nor palpable. Heart sounds present no abnormalities.

Lungs: Hyperresonance on left. Resonance unchanged or slightly diminished on right, anteriorly to anterior axillary line; dullness on right posteriorly, ending anteriorly at anterior axillary line. Fremitus absent over dull area and increased over rest of lungs. Egophony on left anteriorly to anterior axillary line. The line of demarkation remains fixed even when patient lies on left side. Breath sounds absent over dull area. Breathing increased over rest of lung with sounds harsh and expiration prolonged.

Abdomen: Presents nothing abnormal.

Extremities: Greatly wasted, no edema.

Ward Notes.—Nov. 28. Patient admitted in a very low state of vitality. Pulse almost imperceptible. Heart sound rapid and weak. Breathing short and rather labored.

Patient much emaciated, tongue red and dry, cheeks sunken.

Lungs: On the right side posteriorly there was dullness extending upward to about the 8th rib, and going anteriorly to about the mid-clavicular line. Over this area there was absent fremitus and breath sounds were weak and distant.

Above this area and over the other lung the breath sounds were harsh and somewhat exaggerated.

Patient has incontinence of both urine and feces.

Nov. 30. Patient steadily growing weaker. Heart sounds weak, pulse very weak. Effusion remains about the same. Needle introduced to-day and a syringeful of clear reddish fluid withdrawn.

Dec. 3. Patient gradually getting weaker, heart sounds very indistinct. Lung condition about same.

Autopsy Record.—(By Joseph McFarland, M. D., Pathologist). Dec. 4, 1900. J. H., age 56, male, white.

Clinical Diagnosis.—Croupous pneumonia.

Pathological Diagnosis.—Miliary tuberculosis both lungs. Chronic tuberculous pleuritis of right side, with adhesions and localized effusion. Miliary tuberculosis of liver, kidney and suprarenals. Ball-thrombus of heart.

Notes.—Heart. Normal in size. Right ventricle is filled with firm coagula, one of which is the size of a soup bean, dense and fibrous in structure. It is free in the cavity. The structure of the thrombus is laminated (ante mortem). Left ventricle is normal (walls, etc.) with no disease of the valves. Auricles normal. There is slight sclerosis of coronaries.

Notes on other organs had no bearing upon cardiac condition.

SECOND CASE.

Philadelphia Hospital, 1900. No. 3218.

W. F. Men's Med. No. 7. Admitted Nov. 12, 1900. Died Dec. 13, 1900.

Primary Diagnosis.—Tubercular pneumonia.

History.—W. F., white, age 66, birthplace, Philadelphia; occupation, boxmaker.

Chief Complaint.—Shortness of breath.

Family History.—Both parents died of old age.

Previous Medical History.—Measles and smallpox when a child. Had influenza three years ago. Pleurisy on right side some years ago.

History of Present Illness.—Fifteen months ago he noticed that he was not as strong as he should be and that he lost ambition for work; that he felt very weak in the morning. Five months ago he went to the Pennsylvania Hospital, and remained there for two and a half months. He was short of breath and had a cough. He says he felt much better and thought he could go out and work. He was only able to work three weeks and then had to stop on account of shortness of breath and weakness. He now has a cough. Expectoration frothy and he says it is sticky. One week ago he started coughing up blood. Has not had any night sweats but has lost considerable flesh.

Examination.—General appearance: Fairly well nourished. Sharp features.

Eyes: Pupils small and react slowly to light and distance.

Pulse: Small, rapid, regular.

Tongue: Coated irregularly; clean at the edges.

Heart: Apex one-half inch outside the nipple line. Both sounds are indistinct. Action accelerated.

Lungs: Respiration accelerated and shallow. Impaired resonance at right apex; on auscultation fine moist râles.

Abdomen: Liver dullness slightly increased.

Ward Notes.—Nov. 12, 1900. Upon admission patient complains of dyspnœa and pains in chest. Lips and finger tips slightly cyanosed.

Respiration shallow, rapid. Face is flushed. Cheek bones prominent. Emaciated. Average height. General color poor. Arteries sclerotic and beady. Pupils equal, react to light. Tongue coated.

Expansion of lungs poor, almost absent at apices. Percussion noted over right apex and over right lung posteriorly, *flat*. Over left lung fremitus increased, percussion note dull or impaired at apex. Auscultation, tubular breathing is heard posteriorly in an area about size of palm of hand at inferior border of scapula. Below and above same numerous moist râles are heard both on inspiration and expiration.

Over left apex dry râles are heard on both inspiration and expiration, do not clear up with coughing. Sputum is thick and tenacious and streaked with blood. Has no abdominal affection. Heart is slightly displaced to left; no murmurs detected. No involvement of bladder or rectum.

Nov. 15. See no change in patient's condition from note above made upon admission.

Nov. 20. Patient quite ill, appears much weaker this A. M. Expectoration still profuse, sweats at night, Repeated examination of sputum reveals no tubercle bacilli.

Dec. 1. Patient no better. Lungs present a more advanced stage of resolution than upon admission. Condition poor.

Dec. 5. Patient sinking rapidly, respiration rapid, shallow. Heart weak, feeble and in bad condition.

Dec. 13. Patient this A. M. very weak, pulse almost imperceptible. Hands and feet cold. Condition poor. Breath sounds distant. 9.15 P. M. ceased to breathe.

Urine negative for albumin, casts and sugar.

Sputum negative for *Bacillus tuberculosis*, contains streptococci and diplococci.

Autopsy Record.—(By Joseph McFarland, M. D., Pathologist). W. F., age 66, male, white. Died 9.15 P. M., Dec. 13, 1900. Autopsy 3.15 P. M., Dec. 14, 1900.

Clinical Diagnosis.—Tubercular pneumonia.

Pathological Diagnosis.—Cardiac thrombosis. Hemorrhagic infarction of lungs. Bronchiectasis. Cirrhosis of liver. Edema of lungs. Peribronchial pneumonia.

Heart: Right auricle occupied by a small thrombus. This auriculo-ventricular orifice admits three fingers easily (Fig. 8).

Left auricle contains large ball-thrombus (Fig. 8) and numerous recent clots.

Heart is of bovine size from dilation of both auricles and ventricles. There is hypertrophy of both ventricles and some myocardial degeneration.

Left ventricle contains a very large thrombus filling at least half of its cavity and is evidently quite old, being intimately united with the endocardium. Its center is softened and grayish in color. Rather than projecting into the ventricle this thrombus fills up its entire lower part, reducing the size of the cavity to about half. A second small thrombus projected from the wall higher up.

In the right ventricular cavity at its apex is a cherry-sized thrombus with softened center.

Lungs: Right is edematous at the apex. The upper lobe shows no interesting lesions. Middle lobe shows good-sized hemorrhagic infarction.

Lower lobe anteriorly and externally shows a consolidated area containing bronchiectatic cavities. Scattered through the lung tissues are hemorrhagic areas, infarction and pneumonia. A healed tubercle the size of a pea was found thoroughly encapsulated and partly calcified. Pulmonary artery contained a large thrombus.

Left is edematous. No hemorrhagic infarction. No pneumonic areas.

This man had an abnormally large thymus gland. The other organs contained no lesions referable to heart condition.

Dr. McFarland kindly loaned me a photograph of the thrombus in this second case (Fig. 8), and it is also pictured in his text book on

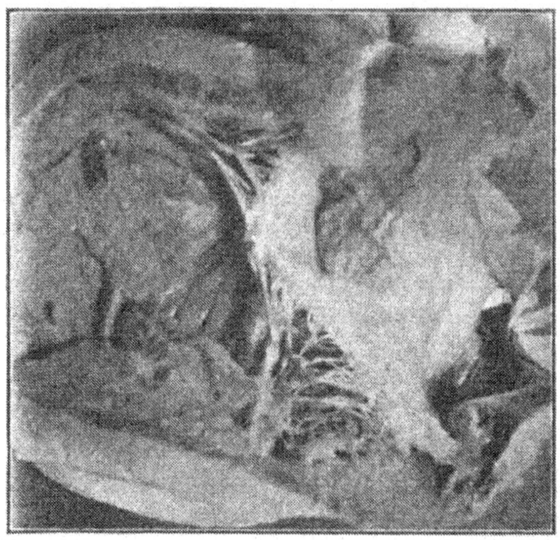

FIG. 8.—JOSEPH MCFARLAND'S CASE.

Pathology (p. 32). This is, as well as his first case, evidently, on consideration, not a case of ball-thrombus; nor does the definition of ball-thrombi offered in his text book (p. 33) give a true conception of these bodies.

In 1904 Professor Paul Ernst[32] presented to the Zurich Medical Society a specimen of a heart of a woman 64 years of age. This showed a remarkably large and fenestrated membrane, a congenital anomaly. On this membrane in the right auricle there was a cherry-sized, round, pedunculated thrombus. He was not absolutely sure where this thrombus may have arisen, but believed the lattice-work formation of this membrane was more favorable for the formation of thrombi and that his specimen is of importance for the demonstration of ball-thrombi.

The case that was autopsied by me had been a patient of Dr. William Wier, of Cleveland, Ohio. He has kindly furnished me with the clinical history as compiled from his office record and the gynecological records of the Lakeside Hospital. I present his notes as he has sent them to me.

Mrs. J. W., age 36, was admitted to Lakeside Hospital, Cleveland, O., June 16, 1908, complaining of severe pain in the right iliac region which came on suddenly a few hours previously.

Two days previously she had consulted her physician at his office complaining of shortness of breath, palpitation, edema of the ankles, chronic cough, menorrhagia, constipation and hemorrhoids. At this time there was no abdominal pain and examination of the abdomen showed nothing abnormal. Further examination revealed the heart markedly enlarged to the left; a loud systolic murmur, loudest at the apex and transmitted into the axilla; and a marked thrill at the apex. There were a few râles over the apices and bases of both lungs. The urine showed four grams albumin per liter (Esbach) and many hyaline and granular casts, no red blood cells noted.

The family history was negative and the previous personal history showed that she had been well until seven years previously. At that time she had had a miscarriage at the fourth month: she was curetted after this but continued to flow for 14 months, when a second curetting cured the metrorrhagia. After this she improved but was never so well after the miscarriage as before. No evidence suggestive of cardiac involvement at this time could be obtained. Three years later she became pregnant and was delivered of a healthy child at term. Both cervix and perineum were torn at this time and were not repaired; as a result a descensus with a retrodisplacement developed which caused the usual symptoms, including a menorrhagia. During this pregnancy she developed "asthma," but inquiry shows that this was really failure of compensation of a damaged heart; the shortness of breath continued from this time to the present. She gave a history of an attack of "rheumatism" in November, 1907; there was no fever at that time, the pain was limited to the feet and absent when not on the feet; the attack lasted but a week and a half and at the time of this examination there was a marked giving way of the arches of the insteps; this "rheumatism" was accordingly interpreted as a symptom of flat-foot. The patient was advised as to rest, diet, etc., and was given digitalis and strychnin.

Two days before admission to the hospital she was seized with a sudden severe pain in the right iliac region together with some nausea, abdominal rigidity, slight distention and elevation of temperature to 99.5° F. Appendicitis seemed most probable and she was at once sent to the hospital. On admission examination showed 6,300,000 red cells, 16,800 white cells and hemoglobin 125 per cent. The urine was clear, yellow, sp. gr. 1030, almost solidifying on boiling from the large amount of albumin, no sugar, and microscopically many hyaline casts, leukocytes and epithelial cells; no red blood cells were, however, noted.

The patient was admitted late in the afternoon and owing to the serious heart and renal complications, operation was deferred for a few hours in the hope that improvement might occur. This did not take place and a consultation with two other surgeons was held. Appendicitis seemed the most probable diagnosis and operation was advised. This was done as rapidly as possible under nitrous oxide and oxygen anesthesia. The appendix was found markedly congested but no exudate or pus was present. Examination of the adjacent area revealed no other lesion. The appendix was removed and subsequent microscopic examination failed to show any marked inflammation.

Following the operation the failure of compensation was much increased and the patient rapidly failed. Urinalysis still failed to show red blood cells. An attempt at venesection did not prove satisfactory owing to the failing circulation and gave no relief from the damming back of the venous circulation. The temperature reached 101° F. soon after the operation, dropped to normal by midnight, then rose steadily to 104° F. just before death at 3.25 P. M. the day after the operation.

Of special interest in this case is the fact that the urine failed to show blood after the onset of the acute symptoms due to the renal involvement, the urine showing the same condition as two days before. Palpation of the right kidney during the operation showed no apparent change.

Post Mortem Examination.—Mrs. J. W., June 19, 1908. Anatomical diagnosis: Chronic valvular endocarditis with mitral stenosis and insufficiency, chronic myocarditis with general hypertrophy of the heart; arterio-sclerosis of the aorta and of the pulmonary arteries; chronic nephritis and pleuritis; ball thrombus in the left auricle; thrombosis of the inferior branch of the right pulmonary artery, and of the right renal and common iliac arteries with infarction of the right kidney; acute fibrino-purulent peritonitis and hemorrhagic pleurisy, edema and congestion of the lungs; general micrococcus lanceolatus bacteriæmia.

Body examined 12 hours after death. An adult female, well developed and well nourished, 157 centimeters in length. Rigor mortis present in the extremities and elbows, not present in shoulders and jaw. Pupils slightly dilated, but equal, scleræ moist, nose and ears normal in appearance, lips and gums cyanosed; skin generally pale, that of the face and hands somewhat tanned, pale and thin. Livor mortis is marked about the back of neck, chest, abdomen and over the buttocks. The finger nails are quite cyanotic. About the elbows are several small puncture wounds. The right thigh is larger than the left. There is no marked edema of the legs.

Thorax: The chest is well formed, long and somewhat rounded. There is a fairly marked pericardial prominence on the left side. The subcutaneous fat is moderate, the mammae pendulous, costal angle about 60°.

On opening the cavity, the right pleural cavity is found to contain about 300 centimeters of bloody fluid. The left lung is adherent to the chest wall, to the diaphragm below. [In the fat of the anterior mediastinum no remnants of thymus are made out macroscopically.] The pericardial cavity is markedly dilated to the right and especially to the left and contains an excess of fluid.

Abdominal cavity: The abdomen is rotund and prominent. On the right side, about four centimeters from the costal margin, is an operation wound, measuring about eight centimeters in length, closed above and below, packed in its central portion with two cigarette drains. The external margins of the wound are clean and adherent, by delicate fibrinous adhesions. On removing the drains their distal ends are found saturated with serum of foul odor. On opening the abdominal cavity, the subcutaneous fat is found moderate in amount, measuring one centimeter in thickness. The inner margins of the operation wound are red and injected, covered with a layer of adherent fibrino-purulent exudate. Just beneath the wound the wall of the ascending colon, adjacent peritoneum, omentum, and mesentery are covered with a layer of greenish-white fibrino-purulent material. The tissues in the region of the lower pole of the right kidney are very edematous and of a dirty reddish color. The serous membrane is in general dulled and covered with a delicate layer of sticky exudate. The stomach is markedly distended with gas, reaches 18 centimeters below the costal margin. The spleen is free, quite firm. The liver is enlarged, deeply congested, reaches 10 centimeters below the costal margin in the right mammillary line. The diaphragm extends to the fourth interspace on the right, to the fifth rib on the left.

Thoracic Organs: Left lung weighs 570 grams, measures 23 x 13 x 5 centimeters. Over the anterior portion of both lobes the pleura is thickened and of a white opaque color. Over the posterior surface of the upper lobe and the diaphragmatic surface of the lower lobe are numerous fibrous tags of adhesions. Both lobes are everywhere crepitant. No nodules are felt. On section the cut surface has a fairly uniform light red color. The lung substance is rather leathery to the feel. On pressure there is a marked exudation of bloody, frothy fluid. The bronchial mucosa is deeply injected, its surface covered with blood-tinged mucus. The pulmonary artery is thickened and shows numerous scattered patches of sclerosis. The pulmonary vein shows nothing of importance. Right lung weighs 610 grams, measures 22 x 13 x 5 centimeters. The pleura over the lower lobe is markedly thickened. The lung parenchyma shows the same general appearance as the left except that the edema and congestion are much more marked. The pulmonary artery and vein also, as well as the bronchi, show the same appearance as noted for the left side. The descending branch of the pulmonary artery, about five centimeters from its origin, shows a well-defined organizing thrombus partially occluding the vessel.

Heart weighs 400 grams. The parietal pericardium is somewhat thickened, white in color and somewhat opaque. The visceral pericardium shows scattered "milky patches" and several small ecchymoses. The right auricle and ventricle and the left auricle are markedly dilated and filled with blood. On opening the right auricle the atrium and auricular appendix are found filled with recent blood clots. The foramen ovale is closed. The tricuspid valve measures 12 centimeters in circumference.

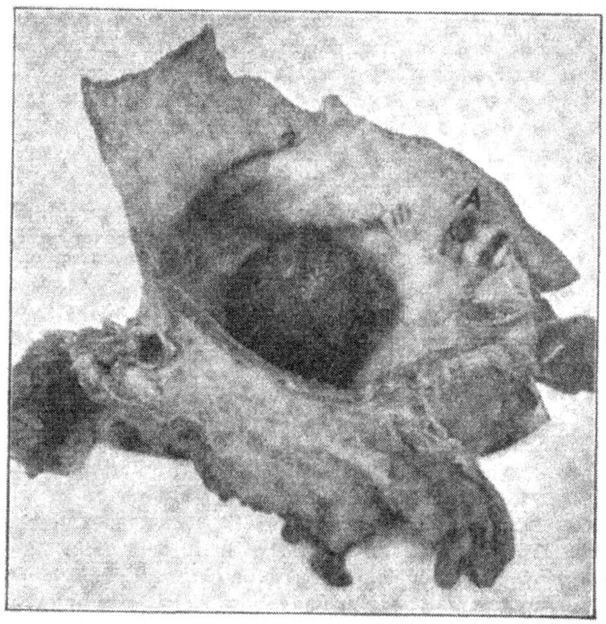

FIG. 9.—WIER'S CASE.

Left auricle open showing ball-thrombus in position, thickened endocardium, small adherent thrombus in appendix, *A*.

Its leaflets are thickened along their margin, firm and nodular, somewhat contracted. The left ventricle is filled with recent soft, red and "chicken fat" clots. The pulmonary valves are slightly thickened but quite competent, measuring 8.5 centimeters in diameter. From the left auricle, there extruded a large amount of soft, red, recent blood clots from the orifices of the pulmonary veins.

In this mass of blood clots was found a perfectly round ball-clot, (Fig. 9) which was afterwards found to measure 3.5 centimeters in diameter. Its surface is everywhere perfectly smooth and glistening, studded with numerous pin-point size depressions of darker color surrounded by lighter material, giving it a somewhat stippled appearance. On magnifying the surface with a hand lens it is seen to be covered with a meshwork of intersecting greyish-white lines (Fig. 10). It is of a rather dark red color and of about the consistency of ordinary congealed gelatin, which it in a measure resembles. It does not fluctuate on pressure but readily yields, only to return to its former shape when the pressure is relieved. After hardening in formaldehyde (10%) this ball weighed 9 grams. On section it was then seen to be made up of (Fig. 11), an outer hull or shell about 2 to 3 millimeters in thickness, which is distinctly laminated and shows numerous whitish points and small diffuse white areas. Inside of

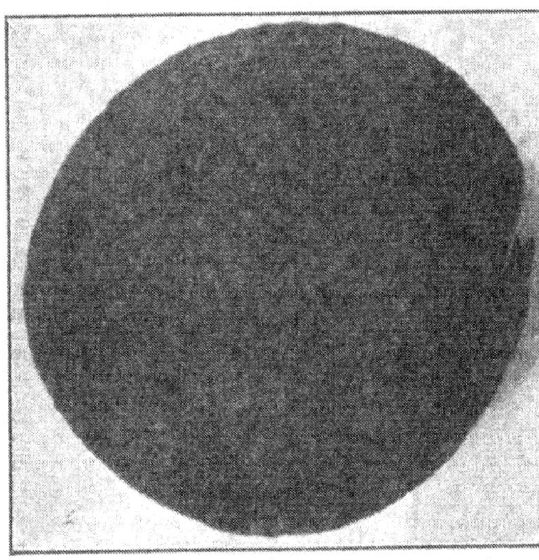

FIG. 10.—WIER'S CASE.

Surface of the ball-thrombus magnified about three diameters, showing the meshed outer fibrinous layer, and the numerous small depressions which produce the stippled appearance of the surface of the thrombus.

this hull, and enclosed by it, is a fairly firm reddish white mottled mass which is somewhat polypied in outline. Its peripheral layers are partially laminated. These laminæ may be peeled off as the layers of an onion. This central mass can be separated and removed from the hull or shell (Fig. 12). Its surface then appears rather rough and uneven. The endocardium of the auricle is thickened and of a dull greyish color. In the lower margin of the opening of the auricular appendix into the atrium is a small, pea size, adherent mural thrombus (Fig. 9A). No other thrombi were present in the heart. The mitral valve is almost occluded, measuring about 0.5 centimeter in diameter. Its leaflets are fused, firm,

4

FIG. 11.—WIER'S CASE.

Cross section of ball-thrombus showing the outer laminated hull and the central irregular clot-mass, magnified three diameters. "*A*" appears to be the rounded original pedicle of the thrombus when it was in a polypoid state.

FIG. 12.—WIER'S CASE.

Showing the outer laminated hull with the central irregular clot-mass removed and the removed central clot-mass, magnified about one and a half diameters. At "*A*" appears to be the rounded original pedicle of the thrombus when it was in a polypoid state.

thickened and rigid, but not calcified, forming one solid membrane with a hole in it, slightly from the center (Fig. 13). The valve projects downward into the ventricle in a funnel or crater-form fashion. The wall of this funnel or crater is, however, quite irregular, containing nodular and projecting ledges.

The left ventricle was opened from below. It contains a small amount of fluid blood. Its chordæ tendineæ are thickened and contracted, the

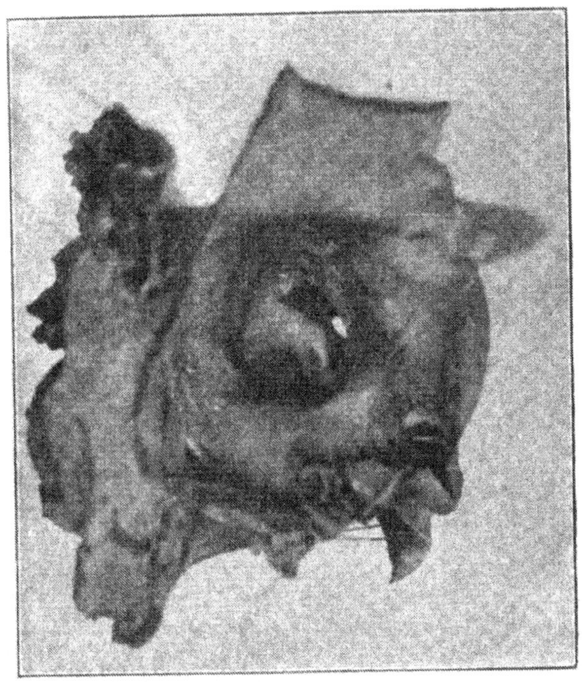

FIG. 13.—HEWITT'S CASE.

Left auricle showing the marked contraction of the mitral orifice, its decided funnel appearance with projecting points and margins.

papillary muscles hypertrophied. The aortic valve measures 6 centimeters in circumference. Its cusps are thickened about their bases and around each corpus aurantius there is a firm fibrous nodule. The left ventricle wall measures 1.5 centimeters. On section the heart muscle is of greyish red color, soft, and spongy. The coronary arteries show thickening about their aortic orifices and a few delicate points of thickening of the intima about the orifices of their branches, but their walls are for the most part thin and delicate.

Aorta: On the ascending and transverse portions there are scattered weals of thickening of the intima, and sclerosis. The descending portion is clear and quite elastic.

Pulmonary artery: Its intima appears in general thickened and shows numerous scattered patches of atheroma, somewhat more marked than in the aorta.

Peribronchial lymph glands: They are swollen, deeply pigmented and quite edematous.

Thyroid not examined.

Abdominal organs: Spleen weighs 190 grams. Measures 13 x 8 x 3.5 centimeters. Its surface is of a greyish purple color, capsule thickened, roughened and lustreless. On section the cut surface is of a deep red color. The parenchyma is firm. The Malpighian bodies small but distinct. The trabeculæ stand out plainly. The cut surface exudes blood abundantly on pressure.

Liver weighs 1850 grams, measures 29.5 x 24 x 7 centimeters. Its surface is of a light yellowish red color. It is firm in consistency with somewhat rounded margins. On section its cut surface has a decided nutmeg appearance.

Gall bladder distended with bile; ducts patent.

Right kidney weighs 260 grams; measures 13 x 8 x 3 centimeters. Its capsule strips readily, leaving a smooth deep red surface. It is firm in consistency. On section the cortex is seen to be markedly swollen and of a dark red color. The cut surface is more homogeneous in appearance than normal and the striations and normal markings are obscured. The pyramids are of a deeper red color than the cortex, but there is no line of demarcation between the two. The pelvic fat is increased and its surface is studded with small and large ecchymoses. It is also of a deep red color. On opening the renal artery there is found filling and occluding it a greyish red mottled organized thrombus extending from its smallest renal branches to its aortic orifice. The ureter is patent but appears quite edematous and swollen.

Left kidney weighs 175 grams; measures 11 x 6 x 4 centimeters. Its capsule strips readily, leaving a pale though injected surface, which is smooth and glistening. On section the cortex is pale. The striations are fairly well marked. The pyramids are injected and stand out boldly in contrast with the cortex. Pelvic fat is increased. Its mucosa is injected but everywhere smooth. The ureter is edematous and slightly swollen.

Adrenals: Nothing of importance noted.

Urinary bladder is slightly distended with bloody urine; its wall is slightly edematous, its mucosa injected.

Uterus: Its wall appears edematous. Its mocosa is covered with a layer of bloody mucus. There is a white mucous plug in the external os of the cervix.

Ovaries appear normal.

Stomach: Its mucosa is deeply congested and shows scattered ecchymoses. Its serous coat is slightly dulled, its wall somewhat edematous.

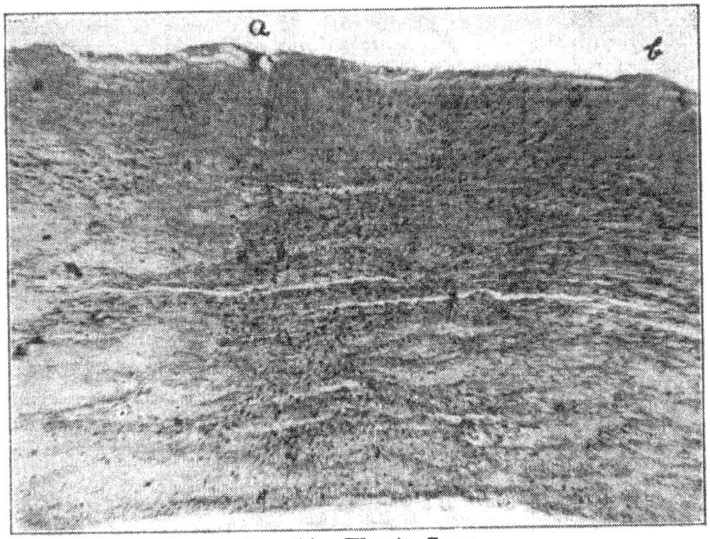

FIG. 14.—WIER'S CASE.

Microscopical section of the laminated hull, showing the parallel arrangement of the strands of fibrin and the leucocytes. At *a* and *b*, the surface ridges are shown, indicating the lines of the fibrin meshwork on the outer surface of the thrombus.

FIG. 15.—WIER'S CASE.

Microscopical section of the irregular central clot-mass snowing the irregular distribution of the fibrin, broken down red blood cells, and white blood cells.

Small intestines: Mucosa deeply injected and red; its serous coat is also slightly dulled and covered with small patches of fibrin.

Large intestines: Partially healed operation wound at the seat of appendix. On the ascending colon near its middle portion are fairly large patches of greenish-white fibrino-purulent exudate; otherwise it is normal.

Pancreas weighs 100 grams; measures 30 x 4.5 centimeters. The lobules are rather small.

Abdominal aorta: There are a few scattered plaques of atheromata, but it is everywhere quite elastic. The right common iliac artery from its origin in the aorta and extending into its branches is filled and occluded by an organized thrombus. Whether this thrombus arose from an embolus as well as the thrombus in the right renal artery was not made out.

Microscopical Examination.—Lungs: There is marked congestion and edema. The interalveolar wall is slightly thickened and pigmented. There is a round-cell infiltration beneath the pleura. The walls of the arteries are especially thickened, some of the lumina being almost occluded. In some of the arteries are septic thrombi. There is some emphysema.

Heart muscle: There is marked hypertrophy of the cardiac cells and some fatty degeneration. The interfibrillar connective tissue is markedly increased, the walls of the smaller blood vessels thickened.

Ball-thrombus: Sections of the outer hull or shell show it to be made up of parallel strands and layers of fibrin (Fig. 14), between which are numerous leucocytes and broken red blood cells. On the surface the meshwork formation can be seen (Fig. 14, a and b) of strands and layers of pure fibrin. A section of the central mass shows it to be made up of irregularly disposed masses of fibrin (Fig. 15), between which are numerous leucocytes, red blood cells, and a quantity of detritus.

Liver: There is marked chronic passive congestion. The portal connective tissue is increased. The liver cells show parenchymatous degeneration.

Spleen: There is marked chronic congestion and increase of its connective tissue stroma. The blood vessels show thickening of their intima. The Malpighian bodies are small and ill defined.

Pancreas: The interlobular connective tissue is markedly increased, as is that in the islands of Langerhans. There are scattered areas of autolysis. In some of the islands of Langerhans there has been hemorrhage.

Right kidney: The tubular cells are everywhere swollen and necrosed except for a narrow ring around the cortex. The arteries are filled with thrombi, the veins are empty.

Left kidney: There is extensive parenchymatous degeneration of the convoluted tubules. Many of the glomeruli show fibrous thickening of their capsules, others show complete fibrosis. The inter-tubular connective tissue is increased and there is some round cell infiltration. The blood vessels have thickened walls and are everywhere markedly congested.

Uterus: Its mucosa is deeply injected. The glandular tubules are dilated, many of them cystic. The blood contains numerous leucocytes. The intertubular connective tissue is increased. The uterine wall shows marked injection of its blood vessels.

Bacteriological Report.—Smears from the abdominal cavity showed single cocci and diplococci with definite capsules (Welch's capsule stain).

Agar tubes from the heart's blood, thrombus of the renal artery, and the general peritoneal cavity gave typical growths of the *Micrococcus lanceolatus or Diplococcus pneumoniae.*

Dr. C. H. Bunting, Professor of Pathology, University of Wisconsin, recently informed me of a case of loose clot in the left auricle which he autopsied while Assistant Resident Pathologist to the Johns Hopkins Hospital, and has kindly allowed me to include it in my collection of cases.

Dr. G. H. Whipple, Resident Pathologist of the Johns Hopkins Hospital, has kindly furnished me with the notes on the case and, as it has never been published, I herewith present it as received from him.

Johns Hopkins Hospital. Autopsy No. 2449.

M. W., age 29 years. Maternity Ward. Died 3.55 P. M., Dec. 28, 1904. Autopsy, Dr. Bunting, 10.15 A. M.

Clinical History.—Admitted Dec. 27. Transferred to medical side Dec. 27, 1904. Diagnosis: Pseudocyesis—ascites from cardiac breakdown, mitral stenosis. Date of marriage, 13 years ago. Has had five children and two miscarriages. Age of oldest child 13 years; of youngest four to eight months. Date of miscarriages and period of development: abortions at two months. History of previous pregnancies and labors: patient says she was always short of breath during her pregnancies but never was troubled by any special edema. Labors were normal, the patient being attended by a midwife. Menses first appeared at 13 years. Occur every four weeks, last four days with slight pain. Date of last menstruation: says she has missed her periods for last six months. Date of first perception of foetal movements: thinks she has felt movement. History of present pregnancy: no definite history of vomiting, some headache. Patient has been short of breath for over six months and about six months ago noticed that legs had begun to swell. This swelling has gradually increased up to the present time. Patient says she has been unable to lie down for last six weeks. Has had a cough all the fall. She had typhoid fever as a girl of 12; pneumonia and pleurisy on left side three years ago; also rheumatism three years ago. Knees were affected and patient could not walk. F. H.: no tuberculosis. Condition of breasts: both breasts small, flabby and pendulous; contain no colostrum; do not look pregnant. Position and rate of foetal heart not heard. Cervix is hard. Question as to whether patient is really pregnant. Patient is too ill for even lateral measurements to be taken. She is only able to breathe when propped well up in bed.

Dec. 27. Patient rather stout woman, face slightly cyanotic, lips blue. Tongue coated, respiration labored, some cough, says she spits up mucus tinged with blood. Thorax: Right breast presents a cutaneous inflammation above nipple, in area about 3 x 6 cm. and one below nipple about same size. Lesion consists of an inflamed base with numerous red points, no pustules, very tender. Movements restricted on both sides of chest, percussion note clear; no râles on auscultation. Abdomen presents a skin lesion like that on right breast, located to right of umbilicus 10 x 15 cm. Abdominal wall edematous. Uterus ensiform and palpation of foetus impossible. Foetal heart not heard. Both legs very much swollen, in some places fluid is oozing from the skin. Diameter of ankle about 23 cm.

Dec. 27. Dr. Cole. Patient intensely cyanotic; mental condition clear, pulse extremely small, cannot be counted at wrist, heart beating 30 to ¼ of minute. Respiration labored, 28 to minute. Patient in a semi-recumbent posture, there is resonance over upper right front down to 5th rib, also resonance throughout the left front. Apex: Very well marked impulse, forcible, maximum in the 4th interspace 10 cm. from midsternal line. Dullness extends however about 12 cm. to left, above to 2d rib. To the right only reaches 4 cm. at the 4th rib. Very well marked thrill at apex and over the body of the heart apparently presystolic in times. On auscultation at the apex there is heard a well-marked sharp sound and preceding it a loud rough slightly musical murmur, most intense in parasternal line in 4th interspace. Well marked gallop rhythm at base.

Abdomen: Very markedly distended, dullness in both flanks up to the mammillary line; walls are very edematous. Transferred to medical side.

Patient was sure she was about eight months pregnant, had felt foetal movement and had even, she confessed twice endeavored to cause herself to abort. She was accompanied to the hospital by a very intelligent midwife who was sure that she had seen foetal movements on examining patient's abdomen and had heard the foetal heart.

When patient was admitted on the morning of Dec. 27, 1.10 A. M., the abdomen was so distended with fluid that positive palpation of fundus uteri was impossible, the foetal heart was not heard, however, and the breasts not having the appearance of those of pregnancy, Dr. Slemmons was in doubt as to her true condition. The patient was in such bad condition that vaginal examination was deemed unwise.

She was turned over to the medical side on Dec. 27 about 10 A. M., and at their request Dr. Slemmons made an internal examination, finding a rigid, hard cervix which also tended to confirm the suspicion that the patient was not pregnant. Bimanual examination was impossible. The patient was too ill to be removed from the maternity ward and remained here until her death at 4. P. M. on Dec. 28.

On the morning of that day her abdomen was tapped for over four litres of fluid, and then palpation showed fairly definitely that the fundus was at least not as high as the umbilicus.

At the autopsy on Dec. 29 a non-pregnant uterus was found in the normal position. The heart showed a most extreme degree of mitral stenosis, which condition was diagnosed before death.

Anatomical diagnosis.—Chronic endocarditis of the tricuspid, mitral, and aortic valves with stenosis of tricuspid and mitral orifice; hypertrophy and dilatation of the heart; thrombosis of the right auricular appendage with a free thrombus in the left auricle; general chronic passive congestion of the viscera; red atrophy of liver; general subcutaneous edema with ascites; spetic infarction of kidney.

Body: Is that of a white woman, 166 cm. in length. Rigor mortis present, well marked. Pupils equal, moderately dilated. Marked cyanosis of face, shoulders and dependent parts. Abdomen is prominent. Marked lineæ atrophical. Marked edema of the legs with slight petechial hemorrhages over the thigh.

Abdomen: The abdominal wall about the umbilicus, where all the subcutaneous fat has disappeared, is thin. The abdominal cavity contains a considerable amount of cloudy, slightly blood-stained fluid. The diaphragm reaches the fourth space on the right and the fifth space on the left.

Thorax: On removing the sternum the left lung does not appear in the incision, and just the edge of the right lung is seen. The precordial space is very wide. The tissue of the mediastinum is edematous. Both lungs are bound to the pleuræ by old fibrous adhesions which are also edematous. The pericardium seems normal.

Heart: Is large, weighing 550 grams. The pericardial surfaces are smooth and glistening. The right side of the heart is dilated, soft, post mortem clot being found in the right auricle. The auricular appendage also contains a firm, grayish-pink, ante mortem clot. The tricuspid orifice admits the tips of two fingers, and the edges of the valves are definitely thickened. The chordæ tendineæ are found shortened and the orifice appears definitely stenosed. The ventricle is dilated, its wall moderately hypertrophied, averaging about 5 mm. in thickness. The pulmonary valves seem normal. The left auricle is dilated, its wall hypertrophied, and on opening the auricle there is found free in it a laminated clot, measuring 3 x 2 x 1½ cm. The clot is somewhat lenticular in shape, being convex on one surface and showing on the under side a depression. There is about the more striated clot a small amount of post mortem dark red soft clot. The ante mortem clot has a comparatively smooth surface, and there is no rough point on it, suggesting a point of attachment to the wall of the auricle. The auricular wall also is smooth throughout. The clot fits very well the orifice of the appendage of the auricle and possibly was released from the same during the handling of the heart. However, on opening the auricle, the clot lay in the uppermost portion near the orifice of one of the pulmonary veins. The mitral orifice is extremely contracted and appears as a buttonhole slit which will not admit the tip of the little finger. It is less than 1 cm. long and about 0.5 cm. wide. The left ventricle is dilated, its wall appears somewhat atrophic and does not exceed 10 mm. in thickness. The segments of the aortic valves are thickened and curled, and apparently would present a slight interference to the outflow of blood, although the orifice admits the tip of the index finger.

Lungs: The left lung shows old edematous adhesions on the surface. Otherwise the pleura is normal. The lung itself on section is of a deep rusty red color, quite moist and showing small areas which are apparently not air-containing, and which are of a somewhat deeper color than the surrounding lung. The lung itself is tougher and firmer than normal. Its blood vessels are free from ante mortem clots, and the bronchi are congested. Right lung resembles the left.

Spleen measures 13 x 9 x 4 cm. and weighs 220 grams. The capsule is slightly thickened and adherent to the diaphragm. On section the fibrous framework is slightly increased, pulp excessive in amount, and of a dark purplish-brown color, Malpighian corpuscles small, but distinctly visible. The organ is extremely firm.

Liver measures 24 x 18 x 9 cm., the surface is irregular, roughened. Capsule is thickened, especially over the lower part of the right lobe. The edge is somewhat rounded. The cut section is very deeply congested. In the right lobe there are large areas in which the lobules appear almost entirely atrophied, the tissue appearing like sinuses filled with blood. In other parts of the liver there are large, irregular, yellowish nodules which bear no definite relation to the architecture of the organ. The gall bladder is normal. The bile ducts are patent.

Kidneys: Left kidney measures 12 x 6 x 4½ cm. Over its anterior surface it is firmly adherent to the surrounding fatty capsule, which contains definite signs of an acute inflammation. On stripping back this fatty capsule there are found on section of the kidney several irregular, yellowish areas surrounded by areas of congestion and hemorrhage. These yellow areas are much softened and are adherent to the tissue above. On section of the kidney one finds these yellow areas to extend into the substance of the kidney as opaque, yellowish areas, surrounded by a dark purplish red halo. The largest of these infarcts is about 4 cm. long by about 2 cm. wide. Except over the areas of infarction, the capsule strips fairly easily, being, however, somewhat adherent over a few, small depressed areas. The cortex is slightly wider than normal, and of a somewhat rusty color. The vessels are much injected in the cortex and medulla. Right kidney measures 12½ x 5½ x 4 cm.; resembles the left in general particulars except that it does not contain any areas of infarction.

Stomach shows marked congestion, also submucous hemorrhages, and the surface is thickly coated with mucus. There do not appear to be any areas of erosion or of ulceration.

Pancreas is deeply congested, but otherwise appears normal. Aorta shows a few patches of sclerosis.

Uterus, appendages: Appear normal except for congestion and slight uterine hemorrhage.

Intestine is injected throughout its length and shows numerous small hemorrhages at the tips of the transverse folds. Otherwise the intestine is normal.

***Microscopical Notes.*—Heart: Fibres are large, enormous nuclei, fragmented. Interstitial tissue is somewhat increased in patches.**

Lungs show chronic passive congestion.

Liver shows marked chronic passive congestion, also focal necroses of liver cells infiltrated with polymorphonuclear white blood cells. Section No. 2 shows also coarse bands of connective tissue crossing liver and including compressed cells in its meshes.

Spleen shows congestion of vessels and pulp.

Kidneys: Tubules show swollen, granular, epithelial cells. There is congestion of vessels and glomeruli, dilatation of glomerular capsular spaces with albuminous precipitate, slight increase in interstitial tissue. Section No. 2 shows anæmic infarction.

Pancreas shows slight chronic interstitial pancreatitis.

Perirenal tissues show an acute inflammatory exudate.

Breast shows inactive state of gland, leucocytic thrombus in neighboring tissue.

Dr. G. Y. Rusk[33] has recently reported a "ball-thrombus in an aneurysmal dilitation of the ventricle." I have endeavored to secure further details of this case, but so far have not been successful.

Summary of the Cases.

Enumeration.—It may be seen from the attached table that, including the additional cases which I have here presented, I have been able to collect 35 cases of loose thrombi found in the heart. In 20 of the cases (Wood, Cady, Van der Byl, Ogle, Macleod, Hertz's two, Osler's two, Arnold, v. Ziemssen, Redtenbacher, Krumbholz, Stange, Tauber, Löhlein, McFarland, Wier, and Bunting), there is a satisfactory clinical history. In seven of the cases (Legg's second, v. Recklinghausen's two, Fürbringer, Rosenbach, Schmorl, and Rusk), the clinical history is very short and incomplete. In six of the cases (Curshmann's three and Eichorst's three), it is only stated that the cases had been seen. It is possible that some of these cases had already been reported. In two of the cases (Legg's first and Wadsworth), the patient was not seen until after death.

Sources of the Cases.—Scotland, 2; England, 4; Canada, 1; United States of America, 7; Germany, 21.

Sex.—In 21 of the cases the sex is specified. Of that number 12 were females, 9 were males.

No.	Date.	Author and Source.	Sex.	Age.	Occupation.	Status.	Duration of Heart Affection.	Character of Exitus.	Condition of Mitral Valve.
1	1814	Wood: Edinb. M. & S. J., 1814, X, 50.	F.	15 yrs.		Thin, pale.	About 3 yrs.	Gradual.	"Much thickened [illegible] quite opaque; [illegible] manently con[illegible] ing the open[illegible] from the [illegible] into a small oval [illegible] sure not admitt[illegible] the tip of the [illegible] finger."
2	1856	Cady: Boston M. & S. J., 1856, LIII, 477.	M.	2 yrs.		Slightly emaciated.		Comparatively slow, 12 hours.	
3	1858	Van der Byl: Trans. Path. Soc., London, 1858, IX, 89.	F.	25 yrs.			About 12 mos.	Very sudden.	Measured 4 inches in diameter.
4	1863	Ogle: *Ibid.*, 1863, XIV, 127.	F.	43 yrs.			About 11 wks., apparently.		Reduced by thickening and calcareous deposits in its elements to a button-hole shaped aperture.
5	1877	Legg: *Ibid.*, 1878, XXIX, 49.	M.	22 yrs.		Well nourished; face slightly cyanotic.	Brought dead into St. Bartholomew's Hospital and examined 25 hours after death.	Sudden.	Mere chink, scarcely admitting tip of man's forefinger; beset with granulations.
6	1877	Legg: *Ibid.*, 1878, XXIX, 49.	F.	43 yrs.			Under observation 15 days.	Slow.	Greatly contracted so as not to admit more than the tip of the finger.
7	1882	Macleod: Edinb. M. J., 1883, 696.	M.	27 yrs.		Recovering from wound. Low grade of health.	Under observation 7 days.	Slow.	

Character of Free-Thrombus.							Signs of Former Attachment.	Remarks.
Form.	Size.	Weight.	Surface.	Consistency.	Situation.	Section.		
Completely spherical.	More than 1¼ inches in diameter.		Everywhere smooth and polished.	Firm but elastic.	Left auricle.	An outer sac of 2 to 3 mm. in thickness; formed of a number of firm laminæ; easily separated from each other and surrounding an irregular clotted mass.	Not present.	There was a second, irregular-shaped loose clot also present and lying over the mitral orifice and a third of rough and irregular shape.
Cylindrical.	1 x ½ inches.			Rather solid.	Right auricle.			This case in some respects resembles the case of Macleod.
Irregular.	Pigeon's egg.		Shaggy.	Apparently soft.	Left auricle.	Apparently soft center.	Present.	From the description it is quite evident that this thrombus was detached only a short time before death. Death was considered due to mitral embolism.
Spherical.	Large.	4 drachms.	Uniformly granulated with two indentation marks.	Solid throughout.	Left auricle.	Composed of friable fibrinous inner substance with a distinctly laminated and darker colored circumference.	Present.	The picture of this thrombus and its situation is the first and one of the best found in the literature.
Irregularly oval.	About size of pullet's egg, 15 x 30 mm.		Gray and granular ribbed.		Left auricle.		Present.	This case showed two balls of about the same character and size except that one showed a surface markedly resembling a broken-off end of the auricular thrombus. Legg discusses a possible ball-valve action.
Round.	1½ inches in diameter.		Very smooth.	Elastic.	Left auricle.		None.	As noted by Welch, Legg had a clear conception of the formation of these thrombi and was the first to argue that they might act as "ball-valves."
	Half as large again as a walnut.			Very firm, almost cartilaginous.	Right auricle.			This case, apparently, has had the widest circulation and has been known by a larger number of physicians than any other case of these loose thrombi in the heart that has been reported.

No.	Date.	Author and Source.	Sex.	Age.	Occupation.	Status.	Duration of Heart Affection.	Character of Exitus.	Condition of Mitral Valve.
8 9	1883	v. Recklinghausen: Handb. d. allg. Path. d. Kreislaufs, etc., 1893; Deutsches Arch. f. klin. Med., 1885, XXXVII, 495.	Two cases with no history. (In a second article it is stated that these cases were examined at least twice a day but at no time showed any symptoms that pointed to an occlusion of the mitral valve by the thrombus.)						Extreme stenosis; contracted to the size of the tip of the little finger.
10	1885	Hertz: Deutsches Arch. f. klin. Med., 1885, XXXVII, 74.	M.	23 yrs.	Journeyman tailor.	Moderately nourished, face pale and cyanotic.	Rheumatism in childhood. Under observation about one year.	Apparently, gradual.	Markedly stenosed, so as not to admit the tip of the little finger; borders beset with coxcomb-like excrescences.
11	1885	Hertz: *Ibid.*		39 yrs.			Suffered for years with weak heart. Under observation 4 mos.	Sudden.	
12	1890	Osler: Montreal M. J., 1897, XXV, 729.	F.	35 yrs.			Subject to attacks of shortness of breath for 20 yrs.	Rapid.	Very narrow, just admitting the tip of the little finger; buttonhole appearance; edges of cartilaginous consistency; fringed with small vegetations.
13	1890	Arnold: Ziegler's Beitr. f. path. Anat. u. f. allg. Path., 1890, VII, 29.	F.	23 yrs.	Maid servant.	Well developed and nourished.	4 wks.	Gradual, with increasing cyanosis and edema.	"Long oval form," 16 x 8 mm. Valve flaps thickened and grown together.
14	1890	v. Ziemssen: Congress f. inn. Med., 1890, 281.					Apparently a long time.		Stenosed.
15	1890	Fürbringer: Deutsche med. Wchnschr., 1890, XVI, 505.	Child died of scarlet fever with uremia and signs of heart failure.					Sudden.	No trace of stenosis.

Character of Free-Thrombus.							Signs of Former Attachment.	Remarks.
Form.	Size.	Weight.	Surface.	Consistency.	Situation.	Section.		
Ball."	"Small walnut."		Somewhat bulged out but everywhere smooth.		Left auricle.	Contain small cavities.	None.	He characterizes them as always pale red and containing small cavities. His description is considered by all the German authors that I have consulted as the first to record the condition of ball thrombus.
Completely round.	2.5 cm. in diameter.		Numerous "nibbled out" depressions, but smooth and polished.	Apparently soft.	Left auricle.	Soft center connected by one depression with the surface.	Present.	Associated in the same cavity with this spherical thrombus was a pendunculated thrombus "still fastened to the auricular appendix." This was of a blunt shape. He notes particularly the "funnel shape" of the mitral valve.
Ball round.	4 cm. in diameter.		Elastic integument at one point showing a rough surface.	Distinctly fluctuating.	Left auricle.	2 to 3 mm. thick membrane and a fluid content of turbid yellowish color mixed with coagulated flakes.	Present.	It is noted in this case that the valve flaps were drawn together suggesting that there was a funnel shape to it also.
Ovoid.	Small pullet egg, 2¼ x 3¼ cm.		Greyish-brown color; small linear elevation.	Firm and elastic; indistinct fluctuation.	Left auricle.	Probably central softening.	None.	The funnel appearance of the mitral orifice when viewed from above is here also mentioned.
"Ball mass."	3.2 cm. in diameter.	9.55 drachms.	Grey-yellowish red color.	Soft and fluctuating.	Left auricle.	Apparently thin walled with fluid contents.	Present.	A very good picture of the thrombus accompanies this article.
Almost wheel round.	Small walnut.		Perfectly smooth with numerous small cup-shaped excavations.	Firm.	Left auricle.	Central nucleus covered by fine laminated layers, with fine cords extending to each cup-shaped depression on surface.		He expresses the opinion that with (1) the physical proof of mitral stenosis; (2) the appearance of cyanosis, dyspnœa and coldness of extremities; (3) and circumscribed gangrene of the feet, a probable diagnosis of pedunculated or ball thrombi can be made.
	Pea to a cherry.			Fluctuating.	Right auricle.	Soft center.		Evidently, as in McFarland's and Cady's cases, these were not ball thrombi.

No.	Date.	Author and Source.	Sex.	Age.	Occupation.	Status.	Duration of Heart Affection.	Character of Exitus.	Condition of Mitr[al] Valve.
16	1892	Redtenbacher: Wien. klin. Wchnschr., 1892, V, 688.	F.	46 yrs.	Laborer.	Emaciated; medium development.	4 yrs.	Rapid.	Contracted to si[ze of] little finger; [but]tonhole shape; [mar]gins grown tog[eth]er; presenting thick, shrun[ken,] short, solid, fu[nnel] appearance.
17	1892	Schmorl: Schmidt's Jahrbuch, 1892, CCXXXV, 110.	No clinical history given other than: No symptoms which pointed to an interference with the circulation by the ball thrombus were demonstrable.						Stenosed.
18 19 20	1892	Curshman:	In the discussion of Schmorl's case he stated that he had seen three cases. Mitral stenosis was present and death was sudden.					Sudden.	Stenosed.
21	1893	Rosenbach: Die Krankheiten d. Herzens, 1893, I, 180.			No history.				Stenosed.
22	1893	Krumbholz: Arb. a. d. med. Klin. zu Leipzig, 1893, 328.	F.	41 yrs.	Seamstress.		Sometime.	Slow with increasing cyanosis.	Thickened along th[e] line of closure, an[d] changed into a stif[f] narrow ring, admitting a pencil.
23	1893	Stange: Arb. a. d. path. Inst. zu Göttingen, 1893, 232.	M.	29 yrs.	Teacher.	Medium nourished.	6 wks.	Apparently, sudden.	Congestion of liver, stomach and intestinal tract; slight colloid goiter, hyperplastic knots in liver. Slight fatty change of aortic intima; sub-pericardial hemorrhage; hydrops of all serous cavities; edema of lower extremities.
24 25 26	1895	Eichhorst: Pathologie u. Therapie, Zurich, 1895, 121.	Mentions that he had seen three cases.						

Character of Free-Thrombus.							Signs of Former Attachment.	Remarks.
Form.	Size.	Weight.	Surface.	Consistency.	Situation.	Section.		
Round.	8½ cm. in diameter.		Smooth, brown-red, studded with fine fibrinous threads.	Soft, easily fluctuating.	Left auricle.	Apparently softened center.		The statement concerning the funnel shape of the mitral orifice is also noticeable in this case.
Ball.	Hen's egg.		Smooth.		Left auricle.		Present.	There is a question whether or not this is the same case as was reported by Krumbholz.
					Left auricle.			
Ball.	Nut.				Left auricle.			He notes that in this case the characteristic whirr at the apex for mitral insufficiency was absent, and thinks that it might be turned to account if a possible abnormality of the pulmonary valve could be excluded.
Oval.	Hen's egg.		Everywhere smooth.	Apparently firm.	Left auricle.	Apparently showed an endothelial covering and was laminated.		The endothelial covering for the thrombus in this case is remarkable. This is most probably an error that rose from a misinterpretation of the appearances seen under the microscope as explained in this article, see Fig. 16.
Mushroom or fungiform.	Walnut 3.4 x 3.1 x 1.7 x .8 cm.				Left ventricle.		Present.	
Ball.								

No.	Date.	Author and Source.	Sex.	Age.	Occupation.	Status.	Duration of Heart Affection.	Character of Exitus.	Condition of Mitral Valve.
27	1896	Tauber: Jahrbuch d. Wiener k. k. Kranken Anstalten, Wien u. Leipzig, 1898, 1896, V, 348.	M.	28 yrs.	Asst. railway manager.	Somewhat emaciated.	About 4 yrs.	Apparently, sudden.	Stenosed; about mits tip of li[illegible] finger.
28	1891	Osler: Johns Hopkins Hosp. Rep., 1891, II, 56.	F.	20 yrs.	Bookbinder.	Looks younger than her age; well nourished.	A long time; under observation 25 days.	Died in a few minutes after a gasp or two.	Stenosed, just admitting tip of index finger.
29	1900	Löhlein: Inaug. Dissertation, Univ. of Giessen, 1900.	F.	47 yrs.		Extremely decrepit and anemic.	Under observation 11 days.	Sudden.	Stenosed and incompetent.
30	1901	Wadsworth: J. Am. M. Asso., 1901, XXXVII, 1577.	M.	40 yrs.	Laborer.	"Stocky."		Apparently sudden.	
31	1901	MacFarland: *Ibid.*	M.	66 yrs.	Boxmaker.	Fairly well nourished.	About 16 mos.	Slow.	
32	1901	MacFarland: *Ibid.*	M.	56 yrs.	Laborer.	Emaciated.	About 6 wks.	Gradual.	Normal.
33	1901	Wier: See this report p. —.	F.	36 yrs.	Housewife.	Well developed and well nourished.	About 4 yrs.	Comparatively slow.	Stenosed to 5 mm. in diameter, firm, of funnel shape and insufficient.
34	1910	Bunting: See this report, p. —.	F.	29 yrs.	Housewife.	Stout.	Over 6 mos.	Slow.	Extremely contracted and appears as a buttonhole slit which will not admit the little finger.
35	1910	Rusk: State Hosp. Bull., Utica, N. Y., March, 1910.							

Character of Free-Thrombus.							Signs of Former Attachment.	Remarks.
m.	Size.	Weight.	Surface.	Consistency.	Situation.	Section.		
	3.5 cm. in diameter.	25 grams.	Finely warty and smooth.	Doughy.	Left auricle.	Concentric grey-brown-red layers with more homogeneous center.	Present.	
	3.5 cm. long.		Roughened at one end.		Left auricle.		Present.	The funnel-shaped space leading to the mitral orifice is here also noted. Osler believes it highly probable that the patient died of embolism of the left auriculo-ventricular orifice. The picture mentioned in the report does not exist (personal comunication, Mr. Broedel).
l.	3.5 x 2.2 x 2.2 cm.	8.5 grams.	Roughened on one side, smooth and shiny on one side.	Firm.	Left auricle.		Present.	One surface was flattened and roughened; the other round and smooth. It had evidently been free only a very short time.
ghtly val.	2 inches in diameter.		Smooth	Firm but elastic.	Left auricle.	Apparently laminated on periphery; soft center.		
	Large				Left auricle.			
	Soup bean.			Dense and firm.	Right ventricle.			This is evidently not a case of ball thrombus in the accepted sense of that term.
bso- lutely round.	3.5 cm. in diameter.	9 grams.	Everywhere perfectly smooth; stippled in appearance.	About that of congealed agar.	Left auricle.	Laminated periphery enclosing an irregular solid central mass.	None on the thrombus. Small adherent thrombus in auricular appendix.	
enticular.	3 x 2 x 1.5 cm.		Comparatively smooth, striated.		Left auricle.	Appearance laminated.		
					Left ventricle, aneurysmal dilatation.			

Age.—In 22 of the cases the age is given. This is found to vary from 2 to 66 years. Enumerated according to decades we have the following:

2—10, 1	30—40, 3
10—20, 1	40—50, 6
20—30, 9	50—60, 1

Occupation.—In 12 of the cases the occupation is given. These are as follows: Tailor, 1; servant, 2; laborer, 2; teacher, 1; book-binder, 1; box-maker, 1, and housewife, 2.

CLINICAL OBSERVATIONS.

State of Nutrition.—In 16 of the cases the state of nutrition of the patients at the time they were first seen is given. Of these 6 were poorly nourished or emaciated, 10 were fairly well nourished.

Previous Diseases.—In most of the cases these are too meagerly stated to be of value. However, so far as they are stated, they are as follows: Hemiplegia, 2; rheumatism, 3; influenza, 1, and scarlet fever, 1.

Initial Symptoms.—In all of the 20 cases, of which there is recorded a more or less complete clinical history, dyspnœa and palpitation of the heart were the most prominent symptoms first noted; in two of the cases it is not definitely stated.

Associated Conditions.—In eight of the cases there was a palpable thrill with a pre-systolic and a systolic murmur over the region of the left side of the heart accompanied by increase in the area of cardiac dullness and accentuation of the second pulmonic. In eight of the cases marked edema of the legs developed; in 3, circumscribed gangrene.

Clinical Diagnosis.—This is stated, or there is sufficient data in the account of 16 of the cases for it to be determined. They are as follows:

Dysentery	1
Pulmonary embolism	1
Mitral stenosis and insufficiency	4
Mitral stenosis and thrombosis of left auricle	1
Mitral stenosis	1
Mitral insufficiency	3
Malignant endocarditis	1
Cardiac insufficiency	4
Scarlet fever	1
Pulmonary tuberculosis	1
Croupous pneumonia	1
Acute appendicitis	1
Pseudocyesis	1

Character of Exitus.—In 21 of the cases the manner of death is stated or can be determined from the data given. They appear to be almost evenly divided, 11 having been slow and 10 sudden.

Post Mortem Findings.—There are fairly complete records of the observations made at autopsy in 24 of the cases. The following are the most important:

Finding	Cases
Pleural effusion	5
Pneumothorax	1
Chronic adhesive pleurisy	2
Infarcts of the lungs	3
Hydro-pericardium	3
Complete adhesion of the pericardium	2
Cardiac dilatation	17
Chronic endocarditis	18
Acute vegetative endocarditis on a chronic endocartitis	3
Thrombosis of the left auricle	14
Thrombosis of the right auricle	2
Infarcts in the spleen	4
Infarcts in the kidney	5
Chronic nephritis	3
Colloid goitre	1
Persistent thymus	1
Ulceration of the intestine	1

Condition of the Mitral Valve.—The condition of the mitral valve is stated in 29 of the cases. Of these 26 are mentioned as having been stenosed; in a majority of instances, to an extremely marked degree.

Form of the Thrombus.—The form of the thrombus is stated in 29 of the cases. They are as follows: Round, 19; oval, 5; lenticular, 1; cylindrical, 1; fusiform, 1; irregular, 2.

Size of the Thrombus.—The size of the thrombus is stated in 27 of the cases. This is found to vary from 4 cm. in diameter to the size of a pea. The most common size appears to be about 3.5 cm. in diameter.

Weight of the Thrombus.—In five of the cases the weight of the thrombus is given; they are over 4 grams, 9.55 grams, 25 grams, 8.5 grams, and 9 grams.

Surface of the Thrombus.—The character of the surface of the thrombus is stated or sufficient description is given so that its character can be inferred, in 20 cases. In 10 it is described as smooth; in 4, shaggy; however in all but six cases the thrombi were marked at one or more points by roughened areas. The endothelial covering noted by some of the authors, particularly by Krumbholz,* I believe to have been due to their interpreting the nuclei of leucocytes or desquamated endothelial cells, surrounded by interlacing strands of fibrin, arranged in parallel lines around the periphery of the thrombus, as flattened cells of an endothelial membrane. I herewith present a microphotograph (Fig. 16) taken from a portion of the periphery of

FIG. 16.—WIER'S CASE.

A microphotograph of the periphery of the thrombus, showing how the nuclei of leucocytes or desquamated endothelial cells surrounded by interlacing bands of fibrin might be interpreted as nuclei of the cells of an endothelial membrane surrounding the thrombus. The nuclei may be seen at *a*, *b*, *c*, *d*, *e*, and *f*.

the thrombus in my case which, to a certain extent, shows the condition I have mentioned above and how an error might occur.

Consistency of Thrombus.—The consistency of the thrombus is given in 19 cases. In 10 of the cases it was, apparently, firm; in nine, soft.

Situation of the Thrombus.—The situation of the thrombus is described in all of the cases. In 29 of the cases it was found at autopsy

* *Loc. cit.*

in the left auricle; in four, in the right auricle; in two, in the left ventricle.

Signs of Former Attachments.—In 16 cases we have statements concerning signs of former attachments. In 12 of the cases signs of former attachments were present either as roughened and ragged areas on the thrombus, or adherent mural thrombi, or both. In four of the cases no signs of former attachments were to be seen on the thrombus itself.

Number of Thrombi Present.—The number of thrombi found at post mortem is stated in 28 of the cases. In all but three of the cases it consisted of a single thrombus. In Wood's * case there were three free thrombi; in Legg's * first case, two; in Fürbringer's * case about 15 are mentioned as partly free and partly adherent.

Free Thrombi.

Thus far I have considered all of the cases of so-called free thrombi reported in the literature and those cases I have been able to add. Evidently the facts as enumerated are not sufficient for any extensive generalization. One fact, I think, is certain, and that is, that authors have been too free in the use of the term free thrombi or ball-thrombi and that many of the cases so designated and described in the literature have no right to be so considered. However, they are there now, and anyone that reviews the subject will be called upon to consider them. Von Recklinhausen was the first to make any limitation to these cases. In his criticism of Macleod's case he points out that it lacked the first essential of having a free thrombus, viz., a thrombus of larger diameter than the orifice in front of it. He further argues that these thrombi, which in size compare to the diameter of the valve orifice in front of them as "a dwarf to a barn door," are essentially unsuitable for the study of free thrombi and should be altogether discarded, as he does Macleod's case; for there is no apparent reason why, if the thrombus was free at the moment, it was not swept along by the blood stream as an embolus.

Since none of the cases I have reviewed or presented have shown any signs or symptoms which can enable us to know, *intra vitam,* whether or when a free thrombus exists in the heart, and since polypoid and marantic thrombi may have a surface laminated and for the most part smooth and shining, it seems to me we can now go further

* *Loc. cit.*

in our limitation of these cases and say that before a loose thrombus found in the heart can be classed as a free thrombus, it must not only be larger than the orifice in front of it, but, also, it must possess a surface everywhere smooth and showing no signs of former attachment. Those that do show signs of former attachment can be classed only as probably free thrombi, the degree of probability, in a general consideration, being in direct proportion to the size of the roughened area on the surface which indicates where it was attached. It is unfortunate that the method of opening the heart *in situ*, as described by Virchow,[34] has generally been departed from. By the ordinary method [35] the heart is subject to great manipulation and undoubtedly heart thrombi that are attached to the heart wall by delicate fibrinous pedicles are readily broken off. Certainly, as noted by v. Recklinghausen,* it cannot be denied that such might be the case. It thus appears that in the formation of free thrombi in the cavities of the heart the hand of the prosector has most probably surpassed Nature.

However, that there are a few cases, where undoubtedly loose thrombi have existed in the heart for a long period before death, cannot be doubted.

Ball-Thrombi.

As stated before, the form of the thrombus is stated in 29 of the cases herewith reviewed. Of these 19 were round and five were oval. Of those mentioned as round thrombi, and concerning which a certain amount of clinical data is given, five (Wood, Legg's second, v. Rechlinghausen's two and Wier) were perfectly round and showed on their surface no signs of former attachment. Of the five oval thrombi one (Osler's first) was found perfectly free and there was no roughness on its surface to indicate a point of former attachment. These, so far as I have been able to determine, are the only cases in the literature of true and undoubtable ball- or oval thrombi. Several of the other 18 cases may have been free for a certain length of time before death, but it is also just as probable that they may have been attached polypoid thrombi and may have become detached during the manipulation of the heart at the post mortem examination. Also it is quite possible that, had the patient in many of the cases of probably loose thrombi lived longer, ball- or oval thrombi would eventually have been formed.

* *Loc. cit.*

Mitral Stenosis and Insufficiency and Ball-Thrombi.—In all of the six cases mentioned above there was an extreme stenosis of the mitral valve and an accompanying marked insufficiency. On the existence of this condition undoubtedly depends, as noted by Wood, Ogle, Legg, v. Recklinghausen and several others, the formation of ball-thrombi.

One most interesting point in regard to them, as noted by Wood, is "how the circulation should have been sufficiently carried on to maintain life for any length of time." Another interesting question is why, out of the large number of cases of extreme mitral stenosis and insufficiency that have been autopsied, so few have shown free or ball-thrombi? The second question does not appear to have been mentioned before by any of the preceding writers on this subject; however, it seems to me to be worth considering.

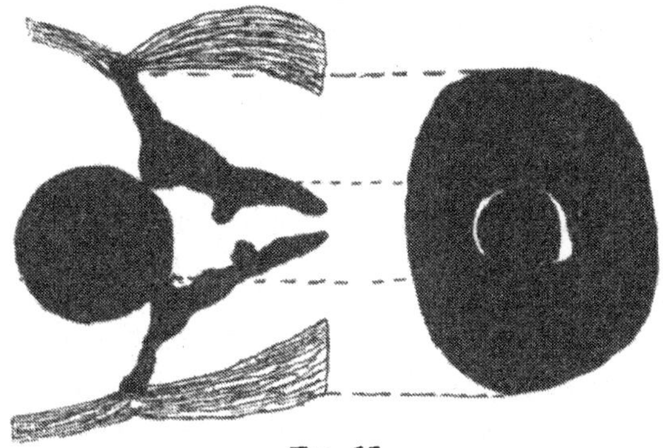

FIG. 17.

A schematic section and plan of a ball-thrombus and the mitral valve, showing how a round thrombus may not completely fill the opening in the top of the funnel shaped mitral orifice and an oval or an irregular shaped thrombus may. This further shows how, if the thrombus should become apposed over the valve orifice the weight of the thrombus and the inertia of the regurgitated blood would cause it to drop out at the first moment of ventricular systole.

Why do free and ball-thrombi not produce immediate death? That these thrombi may act as ball-valves was first argued by Legg. Hertz was the first to offer an explanation of how life continues in spite of this ball-valve action. He argued that the thrombus with each ventricular systole is thrown out of the orifice and remains out for the first part of the ventricular diastole, at least, so that sufficient blood passes from the auricle to the ventricle to maintain the circulation. Von Recklinghausen soon afterwards attacked this view, as well as other views of Hertz, on this subject. He argued that the orifice is oval and not round, so that a round body cannot possibly occlude the orifice completely unless it is pushed or wedged into it; moreover, the shape of the orifice is that of a shallow funnel, the walls of which are soft and, however the thrombus may fall, the conditions are such that the next moment it will roll out; besides, there is no arrangement for catching the ball or for holding it should it fall over the orifice. Lang, who had never seen a case, soon after this took up the discussion and advanced the idea that during the diastole of the ventricle, in consequence of the rigid base of the auricle and the great amount of grinding in its cavity, the horizontal pressure of the auricle was used up, for the most part, and, consequently, a part of the free content of the auricle, together with the weighty ball-thrombus, had to remain behind. Arnold in his report of a case of free thrombus emphasized this view of Lang and pointed out that a horizontal pressure can make itself of value on a clot only when it is lying in the orifice.

These points are all well taken and worthy of consideration. However, there are certain other points, I believe, that may be derived from a study of the anatomy and physiology of the heart that may aid in a solution of this question. In a normal heart, if one looks at the cavity of the left auricle, opened *in situ,* as at an autopsy, it can be readily seen that from the most dependent portion of the left auricle through the centre of the mitral orifice is an inclined plane, pointing forward and upward. This is true when the body is in the prone position. In the erect position this plane has apparently, also, an inclination forward and upward; moreover, a longitudinal section through the auricle and ventricle shows that the floors of the two cavities are as fossæ with the valve opening between them above the level of the lowest portion of either. With a markedly contracted orifice it is readily conceivable that the fossæ are much deeper. I, herewith, reproduce the thoracic portion of a schematic section through the median line of the human body (Figs. 18, 19). While this does not give the exact relations of the cavities of the left auricle and ventricle to each other, it nevertheless serves to illustrate the point which I have mentioned. Physiologically, on observing the mammalian heart beat in the opened chest, it is seen that the atrium of the auricle is never completely emptied,[36] a fair quantity of blood remaining over after each systole. It seems to me quite probable that this same condition exists in the human heart. With an extreme mitral stenosis, such as has existed in all of the genuine cases of ball-thrombus and in a majority of the cases of probably free thrombi, there is a marked stasis of blood and a consequent dilatation of the auricle. This, of course, deepens the atrial fossa and elevates the opening of the valve orifice still higher above the floor of the atrium. Accordingly, it ap-

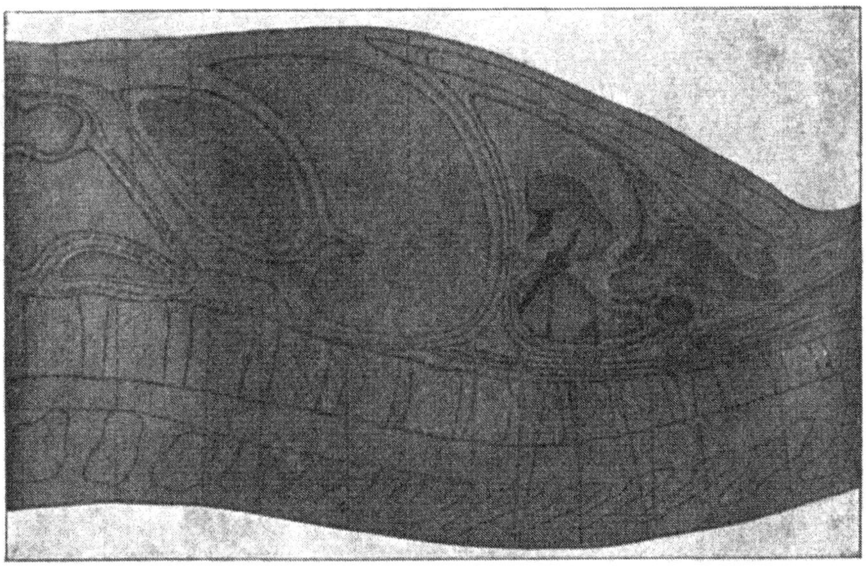

FIG. 18.

Schematic section through the median line of the body; *A* auricle, *B* ventricle, *O* stenosed mitral orifice; showing that in the reclining position, from the most dependent portion of the auricular atrium to the center of a stenosed and contracted mitral valve is an inclined plane.

pears to me, that when a clot of blood becomes loosened in the left auricle and there is the associated condition of extreme mitral stenosis, from its weight, it must drop and lie on the floor of the atrium. The floor of the atrium, being below the opening of the valve orifice, and the plane connecting the two being that of a curve or incline, with each auricular systole the force of the vertical pressure tends to drive the clot up this curved or inclined plane and toward the valve orifice, that of the horizontal pressure to raise it to the level of the plane of the center of the valve orifice. As the atrium is not completely emptied in the normal heart, it is much less so in a heart with loss of compensation. It is thus conceivable that the force of the auricular

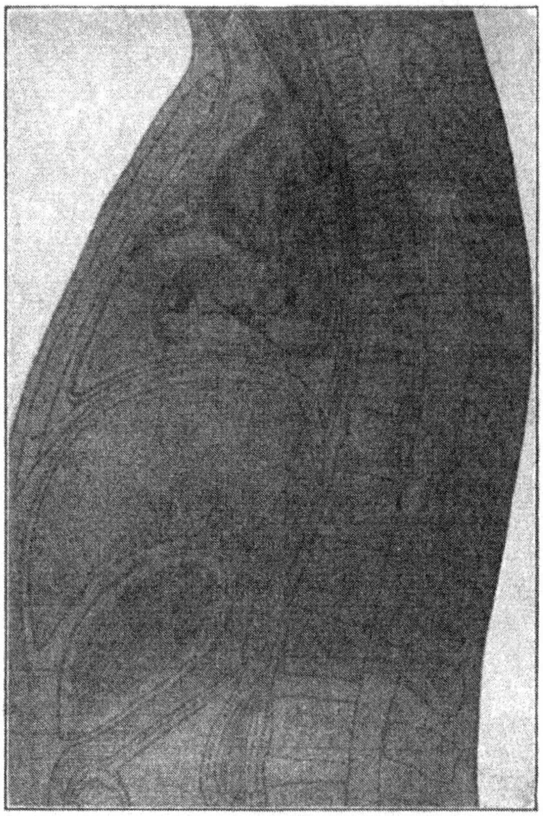

FIG. 19.

Same as Figure 18, in the erect position; *A* auricle, *B* ventricle, *O* stenosed mitral orifice; showing that in this position also from the most dependent portion of the atrium of the auricle to the center of the contracted mitral orifice is an inclined plane.

contraction and the suction of the blood through the contracted valve orifice is not sufficient to raise a thrombus of 10 grams weight up to the level of the orifice, and it is thus never brought directly over it. Again it is conceivable that, should the thrombus become directly apposed over the orifice, the inertia of its weight and the fact (as mentioned by v. Recklinghausen and as is evident to any one who has seen a genuiue case) that the projections and prominences around the margin of the funnel-shaped and oval orifice are such as to preclude a complete obstruction of the passage (Fig. 17), would be sufficient to prevent its being drawn into the orifice, and at the first moment of auricular systole it would drop back on the floor of the atrium. It should be noted also that the force of the auricular systole normally, and more so in cases of great dilatation, is far less than that of the ventricular systole; the force of the ventricular diastole is normally less than that of the systole. Thus, the forces tending to drive the thrombus to the valve orifice are less than those tending to drive it away from the orifice. By force I mean the power or ability of the contracting auricle and ventricle and flowing blood to move an inert body.

Can a ball-thrombus cause sudden death? This question involves the ball-valve action of ball-thrombi and the opinions of the different authors on this point have already been referred to. Assuming all of the cases of free thrombi that I have collated to be genuine, the numerical relation between the cases of sudden and those of slow death in them is that of 10 to 11. Of the six genuine cases of ball- and oval thrombus that I have here mentioned the character of the exitus can be determined in only four. Of these only one died suddenly and that was the patient reported by Osler. Of the 11 cases of loose thrombus found in the heart associated with slow death in seven of them the shape of the thrombus is stated; four were spherical, three irregular or oval. Of the 10 cases of sudden death the shape of the thrombus can be determined in all; three were spherical and seven irregular or oval. These figures correspond with the observation of Welch "that an oval (or irregular) thrombus is more likely to plug the mitral orifice than a round one," assuming the thrombus to have been the cause of death. It thus appears that the evidence is that no case of genuine ball-thrombus, in contradistinction to the oval thrombus, has so far been reported in association with sudden death, nor is there any evidence that it occluded the mitral orifice. It appears, moreover, that the more nearly round the thrombus is the better are the chances that such an occlusion will not take place. However that a perfectly round thrombus may not produce an occlusion of the mitral orifice cannot be said.

Why are so few cases of marked mitral stenosis and insufficiency associated with ball-thrombi? As v. Recklinghausen has mentioned, sudden death in cases of extreme mitral stenosis is not very uncommon, and many of these cases may be due to a loose or ball-thrombus. However, until shown otherwise, we must accept the cases as reported from autopsy findings as representing, in a general way, the relation between loose thrombi and ball-thrombi, and mitral stenosis. It is, moreover, noticeable that more of the cases of mitral stenosis and insufficiency show, at section, mural thrombi than polypoid thrombi. As to why this should be, we can only conjecture. In these cases, at the time of broken compensation, and for a certain time before, both of the cavities of the auricle, the auricular appendix and the atrium, are greatly distended and recesses are formed from the main median passage of the atrium. Reasoning by analogy from the action of fluids in general flowing along passages with irregular walls, it is conceivable that in both these recesses there is more or less of a whirlpool-like rotation of the blood. In the smaller recesses, as between the musculi pectinati and in the tip of the auricular appendix, there may be practically stasis. It is here (for reasons that we will not discuss further than to say that it is most natural from the ease with which the thrombus can attach and hold itself to these muscle bands) that the marantic thrombi form and are generally found. The thrombus, once started, steadily grows toward the ostium of the appendix. Polypoid thrombi always project from the ostium of the auricular appendix. It is this projecting of the marantic thrombus from the ostium, in the first place, that gives rise to its becoming polypoid. The thrombus, having grown by slow accumulation of fibrin on its surface through the ostium to the margin of the main median passage of the atrium of the auricle where the blood flows for the pulmonary veins directly through the contracted mitral orifice, accumulates fibrin on its projecting end faster than at its attached base. Whether this polypoid thrombus will be round or oval or easily detached, will depend on the nature of the original projecting thrombus; if this is blunt with a pyramidal base the chances are that the polypoid thrombus will be oval and of a large size; if it is slender, it will probably be round and of a small size. A picture (Fig. 20: from Adami's Pathology [a]) shows a thrombus originating in the left auricular appendix and increasing in size until it has reached the mitral orifice. It is there mentioned "if its pedicle of attachment in the appendix becomes broken across, the liberated main mass would form a ball-thrombus." From what I have said before it appears to me that it would have more probably been an oval thrombus; but the most interesting question is, why did its pedicle of attachment not break across? The only obvious reason that I can think of is that the patient did not live long enough for sufficient

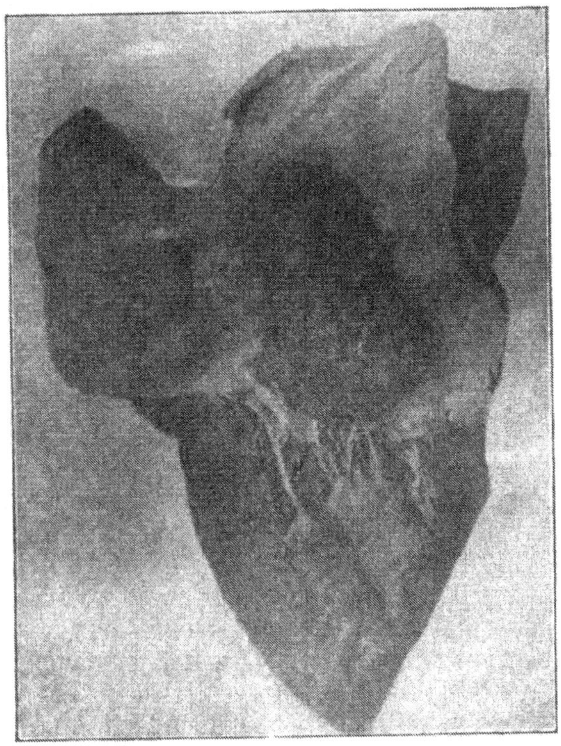

FIG. 20.

A thrombus from a case of Dr. Adami that had originated in the auricular appendix and increased in size till it reached the mitral orifice. It is readily conceivable that, had a marked mitral stenosis existed in this case and had the patient lived long enough, a ball- or oval thrombus might have formed.

fibrin to accumulate on the projecting end of the thrombus. The weight of the thrombus, together with the back and forth motions of the blood, must have eventually broken the thrombus loose. Then the processes of the rounding and smoothing of its surface would have begun until finally a perfect spheroid or ovoid of fibrin was formed. This, at present, seems to me the best explanation I can offer of why so few cases of mitral stenosis with insufficiency are accompanied by ball-thrombi. The process of their formation requires such a sequence of events and such length of time that some intercurrent infection kills the majority of patients before such an event can occur. It thus appears to me as probable that a ball- or oval thrombus may be associated with every case of extreme mitral stenosis with insufficiency in which the patient lives long enough for nature to do the work; and, conversely, every case of extreme mitral stenosis with insufficiency of sufficient duration may be accompanied by a ball- or oval thrombus.

Diagnosis.—Let not the internist be weary in well doing, there are laurels yet to be won in Internal Medicine. Never has a case of ball- or loose thrombus been diagnosed save in the post mortem room. From what has been heretofore presented, it is evident that no clinical difference can be made between ball- and loose thrombi and autochthonous thrombi, in general, when associated with marked mitral stenosis. As v. Recklinghausen and others have noted, no symptoms or signs have so far been elicited in a case of extreme mitral stenosis with ball- or loose thrombus that might not have occurred in a case of simple mitral stenosis of high grade. In fact, after almost a century, we are still unable to say anything more definite on this point than Wood said in the beginning: "All the symptoms of the disease, as well as the morbid appearances of the cavities of the heart, may be satisfactorily explained on the principle of obstruction to the free passage of the blood through the left side of that organ." Accordingly, in every case of marked mitral stenosis of long duration, loose or ball- or oval thrombi should be thought of. Their ultimate diagnosis must, until we have delicate methods of examining the heart and more data, be left to the post mortem room. It seems to me quite possible that with the more delicate instruments, the electrocardiograph, the electrophonograph, the polygraph, the cardiosphygmograph, or some other instrument of this kind that may be subsequently devised, some means may be discovered by which the presence of thrombi in the heart may be detected.* By this means also the observations must be extended

* For an excellent summary of practically all the work that has been done along this line the reader is referred to two comparatively recent papers by Dr. Lewellys F. Barker.[88]

over a long period of time and be corrected by autopsy findings, so that we are still not much nearer the end.

Treatment.—Here nothing can be said that may not be found in any of our recent and recognized text books on medicine in the chapter on the treatment of mitral stenosis and insufficiency. It may not be out of place here to point out that, if the relation of the ball- or loose thrombus to the atrial fossæ is as I have indicated, absolute rest of the patient in a supine position is very necessary and that the patient should not be allowed to get up or even to assume a sitting posture. It seems possible that in Stange's and Lohlein's and other cases, here reviewed, life was shortened by the patient not observing this precaution. However, in Löhlein's case there was a preceding attack while lying in bed, and in Osler's second case sudden death ensued with the patient at rest and in bed. Of course, in the light of our present knowledge of this condition, strictly followed, such treatment would mean the confinement of all cases of marked mitral stenosis with insufficiency of long standing in a supine position for life and with no other end to be attained than the prolongation of the life of the individual for a variable period—a practice that would appeal neither to physician nor patient.

Conclusion.—In conclusion I think it can be safely said:

1. Thrombi found on post mortem examinations loose and free in the cavities of the heart should not be classed as such, unless all possible chances of their having been loosened during the examination can be excluded, or there are on their surface no signs of former attachment to the auricular wall.

2. The term ball- or oval thrombus of the heart should be restricted to those thrombi, found on post mortem examinations loose in the heart cavities, which are of a round or oval shape and whose surface is everywhere smooth and shows no signs of former attachment.

3. Those thrombi found on post mortem examination loose and free in the cavities of the heart which do show signs of former attachment and the possibility of their having been loosened during the post mortem examination cannot be excluded, should be classed as probably loose or free thrombi; the degree of probability varying with the size of the roughened area of attachment, the distance of the thrombus from its points of attachment, the size of the valve orifice in front of it, etc.

4. Those small thrombi, found loose in the cavities of the heart on post mortem examinations, which are in front of a valve orifice many times their diameter in size, should not be considered among loose or free thrombi at all.

5. To William Wood, of Edinburgh, belongs the honor of describing the first case of genuine ball-thrombus of the heart.

6. The origin and formation of ball-thrombi of the heart is dependent on an obstruction to the free passage of blood by a narrowed and constricted valvular orifice of the heart.

7. All cases of genuine ball- or oval thrombi of the heart, thus far reported, have been found in the left auricle and have been associated with marked mitral stenosis and insufficiency.

8. That genuine ball-thrombi in the heart may act as ball-valves appears possible, but has yet to be definitely demonstrated.

9. That oval or irregular, and recently detached thrombi may produce sudden occlusion of the auriculo-ventricular orifice appears more probable and very possible.

10. No sign or symptom has so far been described that will enable one to diagnose definitely autochthonous thrombosis, loose thrombi, or ball- or oval thrombi in a case of marked mitral stenosis with insufficiency; consequently no practical treatment different from that ordinarily employed in mitral stenosis with insufficiency can be recommended.

I desire to express my thanks to Dr. W. T. Howard, of the Western Reserve Medical School, Cleveland (Ohio), and to Dr. F. F. Wesbrook, of the University of Minnesota, for aid and suggestions in the preparation of this paper; to Mr. J. T. Gerould and Mrs. F. M. Leversee, Librarians of the University of Minnesota and its Pathological Department, respectively, for securing reference books for me and for aid in the preparation of the manuscript; also to Mr. Henry Andrews, of the photographic department, University of Minnesota, for most of the accompanying photographs; and to the various men who have kindly sent me reports of their cases.

St. Joseph's Hospital.

References.

1. Osler: J. Anat. & Physiol., 1879-80, XIV, 230.
2. Wood: Edinb. M. & S. J., 1814, X, 50.
3. Cady: Boston M. & S. J., 1856, LIII, 477.

4. VAN DER BYL: Trans. Path. Soc., London, 1858, IX, 89.
5. OGLE: *Ibid.*, 1863, XIV, 127.
6. LEGG: *Ibid.*, 1878, XXIX, 49.
7. MACLEOD: Edinb. M. J., 1882-3, XXVIII, 696.
8. v. RECKLINGHAUSEN: Handb. d. allg. Path. d. Kreislaufs u. d. Ernährung, Stuttgart, 1893, and Deutsches Arch. f. klin. Med., 1885, XXXVII, 495.
9. HERTZ: Deutsches Arch. f. klin. Med., 1885, XXXVII, 74.
10. WELCH: Allbutt's System of Medicine, 1899, VI, 185.
11. LANG: Wien. med. Presse, 1886, XXVII, 209.
12. OSLER: Montreal M. J., 1897, XXV, 729.
13. ARNOLD: Ziegler's Beitr. f. path. Anat. u. f. allg. Path., 1880, VII, 29.
14. FÜRBRINGER: Deutsche med. Wchnschr., 1890, XVI, 505.
15. v. ZIEMSSEN: Congress f. inn. Med., 1890, 281.
16. ZUM BUSCH: Ueb. d. Zusammensetzung d. Herzthromben. Inaug-Diss. Freiburg, i. B., 1891.
17. SCHMORL: Schmidt's Jahrbücher d. in- und ausländischen gesamten Medezin, 1892, CXXXV, 110, and Stereo-scopish-photographer Atlas d. path. Anat. d. Herz. u. d. grosseren Blutgefässe, München, 1899, Tafel 20.
18. REDTENBACHER: Wien. klin. Wchnschr., 1892, V, 688.
19. LANG: Wien. klin. Wchnschr., 1892, V, 618.
20. ROSENBACH: Die Krankheiten d. Herzens, 1893, I, 180.
21. KRUMBHOLZ: Arb. a. d. med. Klin. zu. Leipzig, 1893, 328.
22. STANGE: Arb. a. d. path. Inst. zu. Göttingen, 1893, 232.
23. ZCHU: Internat. Beit. zur wissensch. Med., Virchow's Festschrift, II, 199.
24. ASCHOFF: Virchow's Arch., 1892, LV, 93.
25. BOSTROEM: Deutsches Arch. f. klin. Med., 1895, LV, 219.
26. EICHORST: Pathologie u. Therapie, Zurich, 1895, 121.
27. TAUBER: Jahrbuch d. Wiener k. k. Kranken-Anstalten, 1896, V, 345 (Wien. u. Leipzig, 1898).
28. OSLER: Johns Hopkins Hosp. Rep., 1891, II, 56.
29. LÖHLEIN: Inaugural Dissertation, Univ. of Giessen, 1900.
30. WADSWORTH: J. Am. M. Asso., 1901, XXXVI, 1577.
31. MCFARLAND: *Ibid.*
——— Text-Book of Pathology, 1910.
——— *Ibid.*, 113.

32. Ernst: Cor. Bl. f. schweiz. Aerzte, 1905, XXXV, 16.

33. Rusk: State Hosp. Bull., Utica, N. Y., March, 1910.

34. Virchow: Post Mortem Examinations, translated by T. P. Smith, M. D., Philadelphia, 1891, 47.

35. Mallory and Wright: Pathological Technique, fourth edition, 1908, 33.

36. Howell: Text-book of Physiology, 1910, 521.

37. Adami and Nicholls: Principles of Pathology, 1909, II, 62.

38. Barker: Johns Hopkins Hosp. Bull., 1909, XX, 297.

39. Barker: *Ibid.*, XXI, 358.

SEPARATE MONOGRAPHS REPRINTED FROM THE JOHNS HOPKINS HOSPITAL REPORTS.

Studies in Dermatology. By T. C. GILCHRIST, M. D., and EMMET RIXFORD, M. D. 164 pages and 41 plates. Price, in paper, $3.00.

The Malarial Fevers of Baltimore. By W. S. THAYER, M. D., and J. HEWETSON, M. D. And **A Study of some Fatal Cases of Malaria.** By LEWELLYS F. BARKER, M. B. 280 pages. Price, in paper, $2.75.

The Pathology of Toxalbumin Intoxications. By SIMON FLEXNER, M. D. 150 pages with 4 lithographs. Price, in paper, $2.00.

Studies in Typhoid Fever, I, II, III. By WILLIAM OSLER, M. D., and others. Extracted from Vols. IV, V and VIII of the Reports. 757 pages. Price, in cloth, $5.00.

Pneumothorax. A Historical, Clinical, and Experimental Study. By CHARLES P. EMERSON, M. D. Price, in paper, $4.00.

NEW SERIES.

I. **Free Thrombi and Ball-Thrombi in the Heart.** By J. H. HEWITT, M. D. 82 pages and 20 illustrations. Price, in paper, $1.00.

II. **Benzol as a Leucotoxin.** By LAURENCE SELLING, M. D. 60 pages and 5 plates, 1 in color. Price, in paper, $1.00.

III. **Primary Carcinoma of the Liver.** By M. C. WINTERNITZ, M. D. 42 pages. Price, in paper, 75 cents.

CPSIA information can be obtained
at www.ICGtesting.com
Printed in the USA
BVOW07s1006150217
476190BV00019B/89/P

9 781276 466172